WHO READS WHAT?

WHO READS WHAT?

*Essays on the Readers of Mark Twain, Hardy,
Sandburg, Shaw, William James,
The Greek Classics*

By
CHARLES H. COMPTON

With an Introduction by
DOROTHY CANFIELD FISHER

Essay Index Reprint Series

 BOOKS FOR LIBRARIES PRESS
FREEPORT, NEW YORK

STANDARD BOOK NUMBER:
8369-0012-X

LIBRARY OF CONGRESS CATALOG CARD NUMBER:
69-18923

PRINTED IN THE UNITED STATES OF AMERICA

To R.R.C.

685675

PREFACE

Engulfed in administrative duties and missing the contacts with the library public enjoyed during the early years of my professional life, I have made in recent years these casual studies of readers in order not to lose complete touch with them. The six authors, of whom I write, were chosen because they all have long been dear to my heart. To me, what I have found out is the most convincing proof of the enduring values of great books in the lives of men.

I acknowledge with gratitude the assistance of many members of the staff of the St. Louis Public Library in collecting the necessary data.

"Who Reads William James," "Who Reads Carl Sandburg," and "Who Reads the Greek Classics Today," were published in the *South Atlantic Quarterly*; "Who Reads Mark Twain," (in briefer form) in the *American Mercury*; "Who Reads Thomas Hardy," (in briefer form) in the *Journal of Adult Education*. Thanks are due the editors of these magazines for giving consent that these essays be reprinted.

CHARLES H. COMPTON

CONTENTS

INTRODUCTION

My mother was an artist, a painter until late in her sixties, when her eyes began to fail. By that time she had grandchildren clamoring for stories, and with an artist's impatience of ready-mades of all sorts, she soon began to write books of her own for children. Before her death (at eighty-six), five of her books stood on the shelves of the children's room in most public libraries, in that state of battered, used dilapidation so dear to the eyes of authors.

New to the literary world, impatient of its as of all conventions, with a lifetime's practice of the forthright uninhibited impulsiveness of the artist, my mother was not only interested in the fate of these productions of hers, but didn't care who knew it. No literary dignity restrained her from asking, wherever she went, to be taken to the public library of the town, and when there, none prevented her from looking up the records of loanings of her books. But the entries on the library cards were poor satisfaction. "What kind of children read my stories?" she would ask the librarian, astonished to see a bent, white-haired, very old lady claim the authority for those lively stories for little boys and girls. "Poor? Well-to-do? Boys? Girls? Do they ever say anything to you about them? Do they think Uncle Weary was right when he put the sunbonnet on the little boy? Did you ever hear any of them talking about Dotty Jack?"

And to me, when she returned from such excursions, she complained with vivacity, "You might as well drop a book down a hole in the ground as get it published. Your publisher tells you so many thousands have been printed and sold. Fifteen or twenty readers tell you what they think—maybe fifty —or a mere hundred. What's that? Nothing. The old way of nobody's knowing how to read or write and the author going around and reciting his stories was the best. You could tell something from people's faces, then."

It ought to be apparent now why I was personally interested when Mr. Compton began these "Who Reads—?" investigations. Even before that, my attention called to the matter by my mother's frank vividness of interest in her own readers, I had—not only as an author but as an American citizen aware that "who reads what" is vital to the progress of a modern country—wondered at the blankness of our ignorance about what happens to books after they are published and sold. Reading is an organic function of modern life almost as "natural" now as eating. The health of the country depends on it quite as much as on the material food that is swallowed. Yet we know very little about what is being read by the great majority of Americans. And more important, we know really nothing at all about why they read what they do.

Some researches along these lines are (or were) being carried on in Germany by a few librarians, with the patient thoroness and accuracy which is (or was) characteristic of the German temperament. Some others equally scholarly and, I think, more intelligent, broader in their scope, more aware of the social implications of the facts, are being made by Professor Waples of the University of Chicago. Mr. Compton's informal little essays are perhaps forerunners.

They are full of curious material, much of which gives unexpected glimpses into the American personality (if there be such a thing). Would you ever have thought that seven hundred people would recently have taken out the works of Thomas Hardy from the public library of one city? And that among them there would be ninety-one stenographers, ninety-six salespeople, six auto mechanics, policemen, taxi-drivers, pipe-fitters and blacksmiths? Also a poor few—four—lawyers, one doctor, one dentist and three dentists' wives. Not so many teachers as stenographers, by the way. What do you make out of that? That they own their own Hardy? Well, maybe.

Look at those who read William James (William not Henry). Laundry workers, machinists, grocery and drygoods-store clerks, a worker in a soap factory, and so on. As Mr. Compton says, "They would interest James himself in showing how his philosophy is slowly permeating the masses. One needs no great imagination to take merely the list of names of readers and their occupations and build thereon a structure of ideals which James is creating in the minds of these men and women plainly from the ordinary common everyday strata of society!"

And as for those who read the Greek classics—
did you know that anybody does? Does anybody in
your circle?—well, look at the report for yourself.

DOROTHY CANFIELD FISHER

Arlington, Vermont
September, 1934

WHO READS MARK TWAIN?

Within the last few years the critics have begun to take Mark Twain to pieces, and the psychoanalysts have begun to psychoanalyze him. Van Wyck Brooks wrote *The Ordeal of Mark Twain,* the most humorless of humorless books, to prove that Mark Twain's wife and others cramped his style and made him less than great. Bernard DeVoto wrote *Mark Twain's America,* a staccato, machine-gun book, to prove that Van Wyck Brooks is an ass and that the West, in which Mark Twain lived his early years, made him what he was.

In spite of a long, intense interest in Mark Twain, these two books bored me. I believe they would have bored Mark Twain. What he would have said about them would not have bored us.

However, the reading of *The Ordeal of Mark Twain* and *Mark Twain's America* suggested to me to find out whether people are reading Mark Twain now, whether he is retaining the wide popularity that he had when he was living. Accordingly, I examined the records of 3,289 Mark Twain adult readers in the St. Louis Public Library. These do not include thousands of children reading Mark Twain. Without anticipating what the investigation showed in detail, I am sure I am safe in saying, if St. Louis is typical of other parts of America, that Mark Twain is today the most widely read American author, living or dead. By this I mean that, if it were possible to question all persons in the United States who can be classed as book readers, as to American authors, some of whose books they had read, Mark Twain's name would top the list.

It is quite possible that a few American writers of popular Western, detective, and romantic love stories are read in more volume than Mark Twain, but each of these writers has a comparatively limited clientèle, whose appetite for that kind of reading is insatiable. If Zane Grey, for example, could write a new thriller every week, his special following would devour it and ask for more. My statement as to Mark Twain's popularity is based in part on library statistics, but more particularly on the opinion expressed to me by librarians who have an intimate knowledge of what people read. The following table is illuminating:

Number of Copies, Including Duplicates, in the *St. Louis Public Library,* of the *Books of Authors Named*

Mark Twain	Sinclair Lewis	Henry James	Ernest Hemingway
1,897	472	388	30

It may be thought that, because Mark Twain was born in Missouri, spent his early years there and placed the scenes of many of his books there, he would naturally be more widely read in Missouri than in other states. My knowledge of reading tastes in libraries far distant from St. Louis, however, does not lead me to believe that his popularity depends to any extent upon locality. This opinion is confirmed by the replies received from the Newark, Chicago, and New York public libraries in response to inquiries regarding the number of copies on their shelves of the books of the authors just listed:

Newark Public Library

Mark Twain	Sinclair Lewis	Henry James	Ernest Hemingway
1,341*	310	107	101

_____
* In main library 441; in children's room, 900.

Chicago Public Library*

Mark Twain	Sinclair Lewis	Henry James	Ernest Hemingway
2,655	1,105	200	130

_____
* Figures for the Chicago Public Library represent not actual copies but "a guess as to the number of copies we should probably carry now if we could afford to buy them."

New York Public Library*

Mark Twain	Sinclair Lewis	Henry James	Ernest Hemingway
122	148	73	70

_____
* Central Circulation Branch.

Boston Public Library

Mark Twain	Sinclair Lewis	Henry James	Ernest Hemingway
1,479	290	272	3

Before telling more about the 3,289 Mark Twain readers in St. Louis, I wish to give two quotations, which seem to me to be apposite. The first is from Mark Twain:

> I have never tried, in even one single little instance, to help cultivate the cultivated classes. I was not equipped for it either by native gifts or training. And I never had any ambition in that direction, but always hunted for bigger game—the masses. I have seldom deliberately tried to instruct them, but I have done my best to entertain them, for they can get instruction elsewhere. . . . My audience is dumb; it has no voice in print, and so I cannot know whether I have won its approval or only got its censure.

The second quotation is from Albert Bigelow Paine, Mark Twain's biographer. In commenting upon the attitude of cultured Boston to Mark Twain, Mr. Paine said:

> Of the ultra-fastidious set Howells tells us that Charles Eliot Norton and Prof. Francis J. Child were about the only ones who accorded him unqualified approval. The others smiled and enjoyed him, but with that condescension which the courtier is likely to accord to motley and the cap and bells. Only the great, simple-hearted, unbiased multitude, the public, which had no standards but the direct appeal from one human heart to another, could recognize immediately his mightier heritage, could exalt and place him on the throne.

Why is it that people in the mass discovered Mark Twain and took him to their hearts long before the so-called literary folk accepted him? On the face of it, it would look as if popular judgment was better than the learned. Can that be true? Does the critic accept popular opinion after he is forced to do so? That the people were unerring in their judgment of Mark Twain all are now ready to admit. However, there is another question more difficult to answer. Can the masses separate the wheat from the chaff? What makes a book a classic? Do the masses or the critics decide?

II

Before we take up these questions, let us find out who those 3,289 Mark Twain readers are. From where did they come; from what walks of life; from what occupations, professions?

Let us visualize them, if we can. Let us not merely list them like so many inanimate objects— let us imagine the 3,289 individuals assembled, a small part of the damned human race to which Mark Twain often referred. The damned human race that he pilloried, understood, and loved. We shall turn the flash-light on these various groups of Mark Twain readers and examine them at our leisure.

Here is the largest group of all: 1,268, made up of students. About 60 per cent of these were high school students, the rest being college and elementary school and other students. Books taken from children's rooms are not included in these figures. It might be noted in passing that not so long ago *Tom Sawyer* and *Huck Finn* were barred from children's libraries, a fact to which a most amusing reference is made in Mark Twain's *Autobiography,* in letters passed between Mark Twain and Asa Don Dickinson, a librarian.

Next to students, the largest class of readers of Mark Twain is made up of office workers, there being 230 clerks, 134 stenographers, 40 bookkeepers, 17 typists, 20 messengers and office boys, 6 dictaphone operators, and 35 accountants.

Salesmen and saleswomen number 175, and engineers 55, of whom 28 are professional.

Another very different group of readers consists of those having to do with automobiles, numbering 65, including dealers, bus drivers, auto mechanics, filling station attendants. Chauffeurs alone number 18.

Yet another group of readers is made up of 23 merchants, 8 bakers, 12 barbers, 7 beauty shop operators, 6 butchers, 16 grocers, 17 druggists, and 5 jewelers.

A group of skilled workmen consists of 37 carpenters and contractors, 17 decorators and designers, 13 draftsmen, 34 electricians, 9 bricklayers, and 20 painters and paper-hangers.

The professional group numbers 102 teachers, 22 physicians, 12 dentists, 15 ministers, 10 other religious workers, 13 social workers, 8 artists, and 5 architects.

An especially significant group at this time is the large one of the unemployed, numbering 317. Evidently Mark Twain is popular with men and women during enforced leisure.

The next group is made up of miscellaneous workers: 48 laborers, 44 mechanics and machinists, 3 laundry workers, 18 housemaids and 1 houseman, 5

bus boys and girls, 5 porters, 12 waiters and waitresses, 9 street car motormen and conductors, 13 seam-
stresses, 12 milliners, and 10 tailors.

Factory workers alone, many in the shoe industry,
number 214.

The business group is made up of 13 bankers and
investment brokers, 28 insurance men, 10 manufac-
turers, 14 advertising men, and 21 executives.

Government employes number 20, not including 25
post-office employes and 12 policemen and police-
women.

Finally, there is a miscellaneous group of readers
numbering only a few each, including 2 baseball play-
ers, 1 chiropodist, 1 dancer, 2 detectives, 1 embalmer,
2 elevator operators, 3 gardeners, 2 hucksters, 1 mas-
seur, 4 photographers, 1 poultryman, 1 pugilist, 1
range-rider, and 1 ship pilot.

Now we come to the question whether these
readers, as represented here in motley array, dis-
criminate and know which are the greatest of Mark
Twain's books. If their reading is a test, they do
choose the great from the less great. I shall demon-
strate this by telling you the number of readers of
each of Mark Twain's principal works.

First comes *Huckleberry Finn* with 657 readers,
which almost universally is conceded to be Mark
Twain's greatest book. A quotation will recall its
flavor:

But I reckon, I got to light out for the territory
ahead of the rest, because Aunt Sally, she's going to
adopt me and sivilize me, and I can't stand it. I been
there before.

That's what Huck was always fighting against—being civilized—and I suppose that we all have this primitive instinct which makes us adore and envy Huck Finn. Probably now, even more than when they were written, Mark Twain's books are read because they offer an escape from modern life—our so-called civilization. In letters received from Mark Twain readers this desire for an escape was repeatedly brought out.

Tom Sawyer is generally recognized as only second to *Huckleberry Finn,* and it gets second place, with 455 readers. Next comes *The Connecticut Yankee,* with 409 readers, who, I think, have chosen wisely in giving it third place. Perhaps, as some critics maintain, *The Connecticut Yankee* at times approaches the burlesque, but, in my opinion, in no other work does Mark Twain reach a higher rank as a satirist. The following quotation from the book is fitting for the widely varied group of Mark Twain readers:

The master minds of all nations, in all ages have sprung in affluent multitude from the mass of the nation, only—not from its privileged classes; and so, no matter what the nation's intellectual grade was, whether high or low, the bulk of its ability was in the long ranks of its nameless and its poor.

Innocents Abroad, the first of Mark Twain's travel books and the one that Albert Bigelow Paine believes to be his best, has 382 readers, coming next on the list.

Pudd'n'head Wilson follows, with 327 readers. I was surprised at this large number, but pleased, for the character of Pudd'n'head Wilson has always appealed to me strongly. I can imagine that Mark

Twain was especially fond of Pudd'n'head Wilson.
The effect of an insignificant event like Pudd'n'head's
half dog story ruining his life is typical of Mark
Twain's later philosophy, as illustrated more directly
in *The Mysterious Stranger*. It is not difficult to
choose a quotation for the readers of *Pudd'n'head
Wilson* from his calendar : "Nothing needs reforming
as other people's habits."

Life on the Mississippi has *279* readers, not so
many as would be expected in St. Louis.

Joan of Arc, the book that Mark Twain himself
considered his best, has *271* readers. It will never be
as widely read as others of his works, but it will
always remain one of the most beautiful pictures in
literature of that mystical being called Joan of Arc.

The list of other of Mark Twain's books, with
the number of readers for each title, is interesting in
itself. I shall comment on only a few of them :

Tramp Abroad 221
American Claimant 189
Man That Corrupted Hadleyburg 160
Roughing It 138
Tom Sawyer Abroad 131
Following the Equator 119
Christian Science 115
Mysterious Stranger 111
Autobiography 92
Sketches 92
What Is Man? 35
Adam and Eve 23
Gilded Age 8

Roughing It, on its merits, deserves more readers
than 138. I am much surprised that *The Gilded Age*

has only 8 readers, the book in which Charles Dudley
Warner collaborated with Mark Twain.   In this book
appears   the   inimitable   Colonel   Sellars,   the   best
example   in   all   American   literature   of   the   get-rich-
quick pioneer.

Following the Equator is to me one of the most
interesting of Mark Twain's books, altho I can understand why it had only 119 readers.   It is the most
pessimistic   of   all   Mark   Twain's   travel   books.   A
quotation   for   these   119   readers   is   one   of   Mark
Twain's observations on old age:

Seventy is old enough—after that, there is too much
risk.   Youth and gaiety might vanish any day—and then
what is left?   Death in life; death without its privileges,
death without its benefits.

Mark   Twain   displayed   his   philosophy   and   at
times his pessimism in all of his works, but never
so much as in these so-called minor books.   Three
of   these   stand   out: *The   Man   That   Corrupted
Hadleyburg,   The   Mysterious   Stranger,*   and   *What   Is
Man?*   That these books would have as many readers
as Mark Twain's better known books could hardly be
expected, for their philosophy of pessimism and hopelessness is not popular with optimism-loving Americans.   Mark   Twain,   in   a   letter   to   Howells,   thus
characterizes *The Mysterious Stranger*:   "A book
without reserves—a book which should take account
of no one's feelings and no one's prejudices, opinions,
beliefs,   hopes,   illusions,   delusions—a   book   which
should say my say, right out of my heart, in the
plainest language and without a limitation of any
sort."

It would almost appear that writers on Mark Twain had agreed among themselves to make little if any reference to *The Mysterious Stranger*. It is a terrible book, beautifully and wonderfully written, born out of intensity of feeling. No book ever moved me so deeply, and I like to feel that these 111 readers of *The Mysterious Stranger* were moved deeply by such passages as this:

For your race, in its poverty, has unquestionably one really effective weapon—laughter. Power, money, persuasion, supplication, persecution—these can lift at a colossal humbug—push it a little, weaken it a little, century by century; but only laughter can blow it to rags and atoms at a blast. Against the assault of laughter nothing can stand. You are always fussing and fighting with your other weapons. Do you ever use that one? No; you leave it lying rusting. As a race, do you ever use it at all? No; you lack sense and courage.

III

I believe this study of Mark Twain readers indicates in itself that the masses do have a sense of abiding values and that as one measures their taste century by century, not day by day, they can be depended upon to choose books of permanent value. As further proof of this, I quote from some of the letters that I received from Mark Twain readers in answer to a questionnaire that I sent to about 100 of them.

A seamstress writes:

I was quite young, about twelve, I think, when I read *Tom Sawyer*, and I've been reading Mark Twain, and re-reading him, ever since. My father was an

ardent admirer of Mark Twain, quoting him almost as
often as he did Shakespeare. I think I got—or get—
more genuine fun from reading *The Connecticut Yankee*
than any of his books. While all of his comic writings
are a riot, this especially is a howl.

Of course he did not completely express himself.
Mediocrity is forever yapping at the heels of genius.
No doubt his wife, not being able to write or even think
an immortal line of prose, felt herself quite competent
to smugly criticize one of the greatest literary geniuses
the world has ever known. And I think he was sad,
bitter and terribly tired because, like all clowns, he
looked for the funny things in life, and having found
them he was unable to see just their comical front but
must be forever hunting their causes, which are never
funny, only bitterly sad.

But, whatever was his reaction to life's "humor,"
he expended himself in glorious, immortal books.

A salesman writes:

I started in to read Mark Twain at the early age of
fifteen. *Tom Sawyer, Huckleberry Finn, The Prince
and the Pauper, Joan of Arc, Innocents Abroad,
Pudd'n'head Wilson, Roughing It, Life on the Mississippi, The Gilded Age, Following the Equator, A Tramp
Abroad,* followed in later years by *Captain Stormfield's
Visit to Heaven, The Mysterious Stranger, What is
Man?, Adam's Diary, Eve's Diary, The Literary Essays,*
and the compilations of his speeches in book form.

I found myself, however, always back again to
Huckleberry Finn. I could not tell you how many times
I read this book. It is in my opinion the best novel ever
written by an American, and I consider it one of the
greatest ever written in this history of the English
language. In *Huckleberry Finn* Mark Twain caught
the illusive spirit of eternal youth, molded and flavored
it with that rare charm which will forever be American.

It seems to me that all the variegated controversial opinions about Mark Twain's whimsicalities or his philosophical outlook on life are an aside and most Americans lay too much stress in a consideration of Mark Twain the man. No doubt this is due to his peculiar personality, but with me I have always been interested in the things which he wrote.

Let me get out under the stars under that old raft with Huck Finn and nigger Jim, and what do I care then if it is said that Mark Twain was an old, disappointed, disillusioned, pessimistic individual, or that his wife entertained straight-laced ideas! Mark Twain wrote *Huckleberry Finn* and to me he is for that reason one with the literary immortals. All the rest of what he wrote, said or did does not matter very much in the light of that great achievement. I rather fancy that this will be the opinion of a great cross-section of your readers.

A domestic helper:

I first became interested in Mark Twain's works at about the age of ten, when I was told that Mark Twain had once worked on the Mississippi River government boats. My childhood home is about a mile and a half from the river, and near Ste. Genevieve. I became curious, and eager to find out as to what such a man would write about. A kindly neighbor lent me some books by Mark Twain, such as: *Adventures of Tom Sawyer* and *Huckleberry Finn, Pudd'n'head Wilson, Prince and the Pauper, Tramp Abroad.* Later upon coming to the city, I took advantage of the wonderful libraries, and read more of Mark Twain's books, as follows: *Connecticut Yankee in King Arthur's Court, Roughing It, Jumping Frog, Restless Night.* Of these later ones I liked *Roughing It* the best. Altho it is an immensely humorous story, it is also one full of tragedy.

We could not, I think, have a better picture of Nevada life of those days, than in *Roughing It.*

In spite of his humor, I do not think that Mark Twain was a jolly, laughing fellow. I picture him as easy-going, unexcitable, kind, and sympathetic, especially so with children.

A college student:

At about the age of twelve I discovered in our bookcase two volumes of Mark Twain, consisting of selected stories and articles. I read these two books just to be reading and reread them many times, and, of course, each time with increasing enjoyment.

Last year during vacation I started again to read Mark Twain and read the following books: *Pudd'n'head Wilson, Life on the Mississippi, A Tramp Abroad, Following the Equator, Roughing It,* and *Sketches, New and Old.*

Of these books I enjoyed *Life on the Mississippi* best. I like for some reason stories of ships or boats and this story of steamboats in the early days struck my fancy for that reason.

An unemployed telegraph operator:

I have read quite a few of Mark Twain's books, including *Huckleberry Finn, Tom Sawyer, Life on the Mississippi, Joan of Arc, The Prince and the Pauper, The Man that Corrupted Hadleyburg, Tom Sawyer, Detective,* and *The Mysterious Stranger,* and I am still looking for some more.

I like him for his deep kindness, his understanding of humanity, his simplicity of writing, his ironical humor, also his straightforwardness in writing. What I mean by that is you don't have to read his stuff over to catch his meaning, altho I have read several of his stories over several times.

He can teach you a lot of things in any of his books
which is one of the reasons I like to read his stuff over.
I can always find something new (and that is saying a
lot if you know what I mean). I enjoy the humor he
puts into "Huck" and his sailing down the Mississippi
in his escape from his father and other things, it makes
me feel as tho I were with him, which I would like to
have been.

I first began to read him when I was twenty-five, but
I no doubt would have started long before if I had had
the time but I just started the library since I have been
unemployed, having been a telegraph operator for nine
years.

A chemical engineer:

I was practically raised with *Tom Sawyer* and
Huckleberry Finn, and read them as early as I can remember reading anything. I was born in Hannibal,
Missouri, and lived there until the age of eighteen. I
have visited Mark Twain's home innumerable times and
was often in the cave, acting quite often on Sundays
as end man on large parties to prevent people straying
away and becoming lost. The islands in the Mississippi
were constant sources of speculation and wonder to me.
And I've even attempted rolling rocks off Holliday Hill,
but never with the success that Mark Twain describes.
Lover's Leap was a favorite spot for me to sit and gaze
off over the river. So you can readily see that I really
can't remember just when I became interested in Mark
Twain's writings.

I have read—*Tom Sawyer, Huckleberry Finn, Connecticut Yankee, Roughing It, Life on the Mississippi,
Innocents Abroad*, the stories about Col. Isaiah Sellars,
short stories such as the "Jumping Frog," and essays
such as *In Defense of Harriet Shelley* and the *Literary
Offences of Fenimore Cooper, Capt. Stormfield's Visit
to Heaven*, and most of the commoner read ones of that

type, also *The Mysterious Stranger,* and *What is Man?,* but both of them too far back and at a period when I was too young to appreciate them.

As to the favorites, I still cling to my first love of Tom and Huck. As to why, probably my childish mentality or perhaps merely because my own boyhood was such that I couldn't do the things they did, which makes it all the more attractive.

A baker:

In answer to your letter about Mr. Clemens, I can say this: I have read all his books—*The Frog of Cavallaras, Huck Finn, The Yankee in King Arthur's Court, Life on the Mississippi* is about the best. Last time I saw Mr. Clemens (I am 70 years old) was on Twelfth & Market street in '86 or '87. It was then a park where the city hall stands now. He was with another gentleman sitting on a bench. A friend who was with me told me that man with the big bush of hair is Mr. Mark Twain. Glory to his ashes. If we only had more like him!

A contractor:

I read *Huckleberry Finn* when I was about thirty or forty years old. I enjoyed it very much and read it several times, "very human." The criticism of Mary Baker's Christian Science and *Innocents Abroad* did not appeal to me for I respect and venerate any one's spiritual views and opinion.

The Gilded Age was an intellectual treat to me and I think it could be read in these times we are having with profit as well as pleasure to any one.

I am seventy years old and not very vigorous. Reading is about all enjoyment I have.

An unemployed man:

I started to read Mark Twain's books when I was in the third grade in the St. Louis public schools. My

age was about eight years. The reason I recall the time
is because I have a book with some pictures and sketches
of Tom Sawyer and Huckleberry Finn with the date
of my eighth birthday.

The books that I have read are: *Tom Sawyer,
Huckleberry Finn, American Claimant, Prince and
Pauper, Christian Science, A Connecticut Yankee at
King Arthur's Court, A Dog's Tale, Mysterious Stranger,
Personal Recollections of Joan of Arc, Pudd'n'head Wil-
son, Those Extraordinary Twins, Tom Sawyer Abroad,*
and several books of short stories and sketches, too many
to remember.

To say which of his books I like best would be
hard to do, as I have enjoyed almost all of them. His
stories of Tom Sawyer, Huck Finn and their Adventures
I like about the best because the setting is in and about
Missouri and the Mississippi River and I feel that I
can almost see them and the places and boats that he
mentions.

A musician:

Mark Twain is a subject close to my heart. I read
my first Mark Twain at an early age—probably ten or
eleven years. I think the book was *Huck Finn,* or *Tom
Sawyer*—I am not quite sure which. I do remember
that it was recommended in school, which probably
prejudiced me as I did not care for it particularly. I
still maintain that neither of those are "boys books" in
the strict sense of the phrase—especially not *Huckleberry
Finn.* It is too much of a gem, too artistically executed
to be really appreciated and enjoyed by the average boy,
especially the big city boy. The characterizations, and
the dialects are apt to be too foreign. The broadly
burlesqued parts of the book might make a boy laugh
wholeheartedly—but the adult's understanding laugh is
apt to be more rueful and self-conscious. There is quite
evidently an uncomfortably clear and cynical understanding of human nature at work. It speaks with

Huck's disarming naiveté, or the nigger Jim's innocence —but in those enjoyable pages of dialog there is many a barb clothed in innocuous words.

My second Mark Twain was a *Connecticut Yankee in King Arthur's Court*. That hit the spot. I read and reread that book several times before I came around to *Huckleberry Finn* again. The elements of the fantastic, and our own subconscious feeling of superiority to that bygone age make this book more enjoyable to the juvenile mind, I think. From that time on, I read all the Mark Twain I could lay my hands on. I have probably read all of his works at least once.

It is a pretty big job to say which of Mark's work I like best and why. Probably *Huckleberry Finn* and *Tom Sawyer* will be perennial sources of enjoyment for me. Then *Life on the Mississippi*, with its excellent humor, and general high level of writing. I think this book is the best example of Mark Twain's pungent, vivid style. That, coupled with the fact that he was writing on a subject he knew intimately makes it a straightforward, authoritative narrative that at all times can stand without the need of literary props.

The Innocents Abroad and *A Tramp Abroad* I like also. The hilarious description of a French duel is given in one of them, I believe. I do not enjoy *Roughing It* as much as the above mentioned books, even tho it is an interesting exposition of the youthful Mark's enthusiasms. I trust I do not give offense by saying that I read *Christian Science* with considerable glee. However, in this work, as in *In Defense of Harriet Shelley*, Mark Twain has permitted too much of personal feeling to intrude. However, since nearly all an author's work is more or less a parade of his own thoughts and opinions, that can only remain a negative criticism. In the case of Mark Twain, his personal characteristics can be more clearly divined in his general works than in his autobiography. In this respect his autobiography is disappointing. It is enjoyable reading—but in a work of this kind one usually looks for a more open disclosure of personal "case history." Curiously enough, it is here that one can sense a strong shyness and reticence. In his most genial mood—in the course of the most affably told anecdote, Mark Twain keeps his distance—a just perceptible aloofness. Something akin to the dignity of that impeccable stylist, Ambrose Bierce.

The Mysterious Stranger has often puzzled me. It alone of his books seems to be permeated with a deadly seriousness, and is conspicuous by its absence of fun. Here I must correct an earlier statement. I have never read the *Personal Recollections of Joan of Arc* for this same reason. Glancing thru its pages, I have shied off, because it seemed to me that Mark was too much in earnest about something. That is not to say that I do not enjoy *The Mysterious Stranger*. I do—and think it one of his most significant books. It seems to me that in this work Mark Twain presents a sincere valuation of humanity in general. It is hard to advance any other logical explanation of it. Here again there seems to me to be a similarity between this book and some of Ambrose Bierce's. There is the same cold-blooded, deliberate exposition of human faults as one finds in Bierce's *Fables, The Devil's Dictionary, Black Beetles in Amber,* etc. Both men evidently had a clear and unflattering opinion of human nature. Mark Twain, however, with his greater versatility, wider scope, and liking for other kinds of humor besides the diabolic diffused his bitterness thru a greater volume in milder doses.

That, however, is no explanation of *The Mysterious Stranger*. It would seem to be the work of an intelligent man who sits down and gives an honest, unglossed picture of mankind's muddling thru an existence for which little justification can be found. The muddling is usually accomplished with the aid of qualities generally denounced—selfishness, avarice, hypocrisy and cowardice

—so the picture is neither cheerful nor flattering. Other men have advanced the same thesis—the surprise seems to lie in Mark Twain's being the artist. I do not see why. Nor do I see why a man should be called pessimistic nor misanthropic for having such thoughts. Disillusioned, perhaps as to the truth of the school-book maxims and Pollyanna optimism—but that comes in the ordinary course of enlightenment and experience. These are ideas that most intelligent men experience at one time or another—with different degrees of clarity. The better the mind, the starker reality it sees. It is no small fact that the reality Mark Twain presents in *The Mysterious Stranger* is naked to the point of shockingness for most people.

After reading these letters, do we need to feel concerned about what the critics say about Mark Twain? He has the same place that he has always had in the hearts of the people, and in that place he is secure. As one of my correspondents, a baker of seventy, writes: "Glory to his ashes! If we only had more like him!"

WHO READS THOMAS HARDY?

This is addressed to highbrows, to college graduates who have specialized in extra-curricular activities, to those who have time for golf, time for bridge, time for the movies, time for touring, time for buzzing about in ceaseless futile activities, but no time to read. Probably they will not read what I have to say—undoubtedly they will not believe it. My theme is "Lowbrows read good books," and to follow my theme I am going to display in detail 700 recent readers of Thomas Hardy taken from the records of the St. Louis Public Library.

Do you suppose the ninety-one bosses are Hardy readers like their ninety-one stenographers whose names are found on the list? The boss would hardly have time for Hardy—give him a mystery story or a happy ending. But these stenographers have found time to ready Hardy. All his novels and short stories are represented, *Tess* being the most popular with twenty-two readers, *Far From the Madding Crowd* with seventeen, *Return of the Native* with fourteen and *A Pair of Blue Eyes* with twelve, other titles having fewer readers. Grace, Jean, Olivia, Annabel, Lucile, Estelle, Lydia, Minnie, and Alice made the acquaintance of Hardy's Tess, Elfrida, Grace Melbury, Sue Bridehead, Ethelberta, Fancy Day and Bathsheba Everdene—women of sorrow.

Bookkeeping is a dry, monotonous job, figures, always figures, trial balances. What is there in Thomas Hardy to cheer one at the end of a day's work? Less than nothing. Nevertheless, twenty-five bookkeepers read Hardy, fifteen men and ten women, the *Return of the Native* being their favorite.

Who ever heard of an auto mechanic or an auto salesman reading anything but Dyke's *Automobile Encyclopedia,* or a book on salesmanship? They are not heavily represented here but there are six of them counting their wives among the Hardy readers.

If looking to success, ninety-six salesmen and saleswomen are making a serious mistake in reading Hardy, that outstanding demonstrator of human frustration. An examination of the list does not seem to show many high-powered salesmen, including, however, some real estate and insurance men. They are mostly department store clerks and Piggly Wiggly or neighborhood grocery clerks. The women generally call themselves salesladies. There are a number of traveling salesmen and others who hit the front doors in disposing of their wares. It is incredible that these salesfolks who sell us sox and ties and B.V.D.'s, bread and butter, sugar and tea, can really understand Hardy—at least not in the way our wives do, who write papers on him for women's club programs. It must be a mere coincidence that those of Hardy's works which critics generally consider his greatest are also the most popular with these salespeople. The titles read by them in the order of preference are: *Tess* twenty-two, *Far From the Madding Crowd* nineteen, *Return of the Native* eigh-

teen, *Mayor of Casterbridge* eight, *Wessex Tales* six,
Trumpet Major six, *Life's Little Ironies* five, *Woodlanders* five, *A Pair of Blue Eyes* five, *Desperate
Remedies* five, *Under the Greenwood Tree* five,
Changed Man four, *Two on a Tower* four, *Jude* two,
A Laodicean one, *Hand of Ethelberta* one. Of the
poetry, *Collected Poems* three, *Times Laughing Stock*
one, *Moments of Vision* two, and *The Dynasts* two.
Jude the Obscure is the only one of the novels low on
the list which usually in more conventional circles
is given a high place. Six advertising men read the
most representative of Hardy's works, not, however,
including the *Mayor of Casterbridge,* good advertiser
that he was.

Men who have to do with the construction of
buildings, bridges and railroads, to do with electricity,
machinery and power, seem to have a liking for
Hardy. It is fitting that there should be four architects
and four draftsmen on the list, Hardy having been
trained as an architect, and several characters in
his books, notably in *A Pair of Blue Eyes* and in
Desperate Remedies, were taken from that profession.
Engineers of all kinds are represented—six who
simply call themselves engineers but others who are
more specific, four civil, two electrical, one mechanical,
one drainage, one heating. Eleven titles are found
among the books read but no special favorites, *Far
From the Madding Crowd, Return of the Native* and
Wessex Tales each having three readers, while *Tess,*
the usual favorite, has only two readers. There are
also three firemen listed, one of whom had read *The
Dynasts* and a volume of poetry, *Human Shows.*

There are four contractors, two carpenters, and the wives of two carpenters, one plasterer, a house painter and the wife of a paper-hanger. Among them *Far From the Madding Crowd* was most read, only one other title having been read more than once and *Tess* not read by any of them. Of the six electricians and the wife of one electrician, each one had read a different title.

Including the wives there are twenty representatives of the skilled trades—mechanics, machinists, pipe-fitter, telephone repairman, lineman, cooper, blacksmith, book binder, slater, tinners, printers. *The Return of the Native* is the title most read—*Tess* not being so popular as a number of the others. One machinist had read *Human Shows,* a collection of poetry.

Let us take next those who minister to our creature comforts and demands, and those who make us more beautiful—a manicurist, a reader of *Far From the Madding Crowd*; a beauty operator, a reader of *A Pair of Blue Eyes*; and one who designated her calling as Beauty Culture, a reader of *Two on a Tower*; four dressmakers, readers of *Tess, Life's Little Ironies, Hand of Ethelberta* and *A Pair of Blue Eyes*; four milliners, readers of *Tess, Desperate Remedies, A Pair of Blue Eyes,* and *Under the Greenwood Tree*; and the wife of a furrier, also a reader of *A Pair of Blue Eyes*. This last title apparently is a favorite with these devotees of a life more beautiful. Of the four tailors, one had read *The Dynasts.*

There are also representatives of those who feed us, make our beds and scrub our floors—two cooks, both readers of *Under The Greenwood Tree*; five Negro maids, two of them readers of *Late Lyrics*; three Pullman car porters, one of whom had been reading the poetry collection known as *Moments of Vision*; also the wives of two porters.

Others appearing in the list of Hardy readers are a Pullman conductor, five nurses, a soda dispenser, nine telephone operators, a man at the Information Bureau at the Union Station, two boarding-house keepers, and five waiters and waitresses. Even those who protect our lives and property had been reading Hardy—two night watchmen, a private detective, and a policeman who had read *Wessex Tales*. This volume of short stories might be recommended to any police force; the *Three Strangers*—an account of the escape of a man condemned to be hanged having boldly drunk with his hangman; the gruesome tale of *The Withered Arm*, and *A Distracted Preacher*, an account of rum running, are all good tales.

Men who carry us about also read Hardy. Street car conductors, motormen, bus drivers, chauffeurs, taxi drivers and their wives number twelve. There are also two elevator operators, one a reader of *Wessex Tales* and the other, a Negro, of *Jude*, and a busboy who had read *A Pair of Blue Eyes*.

Even among rough, unskilled workers are some Hardy readers found. They with their wives include four laborers, an ice man, two janitors, a milk wagon driver, a delivery man for a department store, and a teamster. *Under the Greenwood Tree* was the favorite among them, that tale of folk not unlike them, in fact.

The factory workers also make an interesting list. A metal finisher, a dress operator, a tobacco worker, several simply called operators, two candy makers, one Negro man who had read *Tess* and *Wessex Tales,* a finisher in a drygoods factory, a worker in a shoe factory are typical.

I have not up to this time mentioned any of the learned professions, except engineers and they are generally considered a roughneck lot without literary taste. They, however, show up better than the lawyers, doctors and ministers of whom perhaps we might expect more. There are three ministers and one minister's wife, four lawyers and lawyers' wives, two doctors, one dentist and three wives of dentists. The ministers show more than usual literary discrimination in their choice of Hardy's books, especially his poetry. The lawyers and doctors disclose about the same titles as the ice men, night watchmen and janitors. Of the other professions, we have social workers, commercial artists, teachers and librarians. Social workers who number seven apparently prefer Hardy's poetry to his prose, more than half of the titles read being poetry. There are twenty-six library employes listed—nothing to boast of. Seventy-eight teachers seems rather a large number, tho not so many as stenographers. It is, perhaps, hardly fair to give the teachers full credit unless we know how many of them had been required to read Hardy among the many other things which teachers nowadays are required to do.

In addition to wanting to know who read Hardy, I also wanted to know why they read him. Accordingly, I wrote to a selected number asking them three questions.

1. How you became interested in Hardy's writings.

2. Which of his works you have read. Which of these you like best and why.

3. Your comments on Hardy's philosophy of life and whether your own philosophy of life agrees with his.

The answers I received should indicate even to the doubting that along with the reading of Hardy by this varied and motley array of the human family goes a sincere, and at times profound thinking on those problems and dark mysteries of life which Hardy so simply, so beautifully, so terribly portrays. I shall quote from a few of these letters. A stenographer writes:

In regard to my reading Thomas Hardy, I will say, briefly, that I began reading Hardy because his work was on the reading list prescribed at school. The first book I read was the *Mayor of Casterbridge*. Finding that one interesting, I went on from one to another.

His writing is very interesting to me, which might be caused from a serious or solemn trend of mind, a desire for truth and facts, rather than stories of imagination, fancy, situations grotesque and unreal to life,— such fiction, being enjoyable for an hour of light reading.

I have a sincere admiration for his sure insight into character, his understanding of how people come to do things—while other less gifted people stand by and say, "I can't understand why they did that." He makes his hero and heroine human, and consequently subject to fault and not being perfect as other less able writers tend to do.

Of course, this makes his stories true to life. Some people do not like this in their reading. They say, "We have this in our everyday lives and I like something different when I read." I recently read aloud, to my sister, *Tess of the D'Urbervilles*. While she enjoyed the story from the beginning on thru the course of its narration, feeling very, very sorry for Tess meanwhile, she found the end of the story to be such a deplorable one, that I know she has no desire to listen to or read anything else that Hardy has written. Beside being very disappointed with the story in itself, she does not believe in the writer's philosophy as would be evidenced in the story of Tess. She believes that no matter what our mistakes may be earlier in life, no matter how many our troubles may be, but that with a good intention always, and a right outlook on life—that everything comes out all right in the end. This is referring to life and as a result a narration of the events of a lifetime should follow a similar course.

In a discussion among a group of ladies the question was raised who, in the story of Tess, had the most notable character. The one who mentioned Tess was immediately put down as wrong, the general opinion being that Tess was sensual. The final verdict was Izzy Huett as the one; while carrying some weight in the story, she was noted as unselfish and charitable, and being the only one who was distinctly unselfish. This only proves his stories to be lifelike, when a young woman from the background of the story evidences a more notable character than the heroine.

This from another stenographer:

I have read but one of Thomas Hardy's novels—*Tess of the D'Urbervilles*. I read it first when I was just a little girl of eleven or twelve, and of course it was too "deep" for me then. Yet the story remained with me— in vague pictures.

For some years, every time I went to the library I'd pause before Hardy, take up *Tess* and glance thru it, then decide to take it out next time. Blanche Sweet's playing *Tess* in pictures fanned my interest again, tho I somehow missed the production. Then I suddenly discovered Arnold Bennett, H. G. Wells and Leonard Merrick, and conceived a passion for all English writers. And finally, last winter, I heard Dr. Leon Harrison speak very glowingly of Hardy's novels. The next day, I started *Tess*. Of course, it absorbed me. The picturesque locale, poor, lovely Tess and her family, the stern tragedy.

There were two ideas that interested me especially— Tess's thought, one afternoon, that each year she passed, unknowingly, undreamingly, the anniversary of the most important date of all—her death. This I'd never thought of before, it chilled and depressed me. A *weird* idea!

And I loved her saying that her soul left her body when she lay on the grass at night and looked at some big bright star. I had felt that myself.

Altho I don't know much about Hardy's philosophy of life, I believe he felt it was rather bitterly unfair and sad, to judge by Tess's story. I think I do agree with this.

A man who gives us a look in at himself as well as at Hardy writes:

I don't know whether I'm an analyst or just a bit greedy for knowledge, but I read anything and everything. I have always liked poetry—my favorites being

Poe, Robert Burns, Kipling, Service, Goldsmith, Hope and Wilcox. One day several years ago I read in a magazine section of a newspaper Hardy's poem, "Life Laughs Onward." I then wanted to know more about his works, so immediately began reading his prose works. Strange to say I have not read a single one of his poems except the one mentioned above. After reading one of his books I was eager for the others.

I have read all of his prose works except *The Woodlanders*, which I am reading now. I am sorry he didn't write more. I do not care for his short stories. Trying to digest heavy stuff in a short story is like eating heavy food with no exercise before or after. I liked the books *Two on a Tower* and *Jude the Obscure* equally well. *The Mayor of Casterbridge* is his best book, however. Personal experiences in life prejudiced me in favor of the two I liked best.

My own philosophy in life agrees almost entirely with Hardy's. I admire the intellectual honesty of his philosophy; his unerring ability to penetrate to first causes, and his uncanny ability to dig out the corresponding handicaps and compensations of the different stratas of life.

I copied many passages from his books—in fact a whole book full. Concerning myself, if you care to know, I studied and practiced law, after the war I became interested in oil fields and since then have done a great variety of things including considerable selling.

A carpenter writes:

I liked a few of Hardy's short poems which I had read quoted in different publications. I wasn't interested in Hardy as a novelist until it was recommended to me to read the first chapter of the *Return of the Native*. I found Egdon Heath a very attractive writing.

Besides the above noted reading, I read *Jude* and *Tess*. I can't express any preference as between these two books. I may say that *Tess* has more in it that one might call "poetry"; while *Jude* has stark tragedy unrelieved. I have been thinking of reading the *Woodlanders.* The title attracts me.

So far as I'm aware, the dominant notes in Hardy are tragedy, fatality, irony and a sense of meaningless struggle. As it appears to me, this is a just interpretation of life as it manifests on the earth. Hardy, however, is apparently devoid of a saving sense of humor.

An architect writes:

In reply to your letter of several days ago, I shall try to give you some opinion on the questions you have set forth, altho I wish to assure you, in the beginning, that I am a rather poor literary critic.

Hardy first came to my attention, as a writer, a few years ago thru a chance reading of one of the stories in *Life's Little Ironies.* Previous to this, the man had been a name only to me. Afterwards, I read a short sketch of his life and found that he had studied to be an architect. Naturally, this fact interested me and I wanted to find out more about him, and just what sort of fiction a man who had considered this profession might write.

I finished *Life's Little Ironies* and later read *Far From the Madding Crowd.* Subsequently I read *Tess of the D'Urbervilles, The Three Wayfarers,* and *The Mayor of Casterbridge.* This, I am sorry to say, completes my list of Thomas Hardy up to this time. I am by no means "thru" with him and I intend to augment my list from time to time with his other works. Of the books I have read, perhaps, the one I enjoyed most was the *Mayor of Casterbridge.* All of them, however, have been intensely interesting.

I think that much of the charm of Hardy's works seems to lie in the simple and truthful manner in which he depicts the peasant life of southern England. And

to me, England and especially English country life has
always been a source of interest. Hardy's knowledge of
his territory seems to be exact, not only geographically
but historically as well. His descriptions, I think, convey
remarkably clear pictures of this section and its people.

A great many people consider Thomas Hardy a bit
too pessimistic. I believe he was rather more of a
fatalist than a pessimist. And having just a strain of
fatalism in my makings I am inclined somewhat to a
sympathetic understanding of his outlook on life. Inci-
dentally, one of the most pronounced pessimists I have
ever known once told me that reading a novel by Hardy
cast him in a state of dejection for several days. This
may have been somewhat exaggerated altho I must admit
that *Tess of the D'Urberville* ranks among the most
tragic things I have read in fiction.

Perhaps it is natural that a newspaper reporter
should like Thomas Hardy:

It is indeed a pleasure to voice my opinion on the
works of the late Thomas Hardy, an opinion voiced at
the slightest opportunity, with or without provocation,
for with the sole exception of Fyodor Dostoevski,
I consider him the best interpreter of the tragedy of
the human farce who has ever penned his views.

There are more polished writers, of course, such as
Flaubert, Balzac, etc.; more brilliant, in Rabelais and
Shaw, but certainly none more justifiable and under-
standing. Except, of course, Dostoevski.

However, it is best to take your questionnaire in
order.

I do not recall definitely how I became interested in
Hardy, but believe it was because a friend suggested that
since I enjoyed the works of Schopenhauer, I would
enjoy Hardy. When I had read the first of his works,
The Return of the Native, I agreed.

Without a list of his books at hand, I could scarcely
tell exactly which I have read, for most of them were
read as much as ten years ago. Offhand I name *Jude
the Obscure; The Return of the Native; Tess of the
D'Urbervilles; Life's Little Ironies,* his volume of short
stories; *Satires of Circumstance*—his poems are more
than commendable; *Two in a Tower;* a large part of
The Mayor of Casterbridge, and several others, I believe.

Jude the Obscure is by far the most outstanding of
his works. That opinion was formed when I read it
the first time, and confirmed by the several succeeding
readings—yet justly to tell why would almost necessitate
my having the book before me. The personalities he
had chosen to write about are more nearly human, with
all the faults and virtues of an "ordinary" human being.
Both Jude and his cousin-wife-mistress, whose name I
do not recall, are essentially composite pictures of
each sex.

Without moralizing or proselytising, the book depicts
Hardy's philosophy—that life is essentially unpleasant
but it behooves us to continue the gesture, and that man-
made conventions and morals are rather largely a
superficial imposition—and gesture.

Hardy, as I interpret him, believed that man is a
victim of accidents, that judgment of human actions
should be held in abeyance, for we are all both fools
and saints, and God should be blamed for the Devil,
since he created him.

> "What did you do it for? I said
> What reasons made you call
> These creatures to this world of dread
> When two and seventy might be said
> Why nought should be at all?"

I have forgotten from which of his poems that is,
but that is Hardy, I believe. I am a casualist, with
moments of fatalism, and moments of mysticism, and I

think Hardy was the same, as were his characters, since one must have a tag.

Hardy himself would have been much interested in the philosophy of this one of his readers, a shipping clerk, who writes:

I have only read two of Hardy's books, *The Woodlanders* and *Life's Little Ironies*. To the first I devoted more reflective reading than to the latter.

The Woodlanders is very interesting to me, a book which has had a part in moulding my own ideas of life and the world. The very first thing that one notices is the local color of the book. It is said to be one of the two chief characteristics of Hardy's works. The other is his own philosophy, which so permeates the work that one cannot think of the title without associations of his theory of life.

Hardy believes that heredity and environment are the makers of man's destiny, and that little if any of our makeup is due to our self-determination. He shows this thruout the book by the intervention of environment at times when great harm is done because of it. Good is also accomplished by the intervention of environment and the influence of heredity. Hardy does not make as great an attempt to show the type of influence that is brought about, as he does attempt to show what mere weaklings men are in the midst of these two great forces.

His philosophy is pessimistic in its outlook, since man is only optimistic when he has affairs at his own control.

I have had occasion to work amongst men who are hired at low wages and who are not of the highest type. My first opinion was a disgust for the way they talked about things which had been dear and sacred to me. I became of the opinion, since I then believed man to be a free moral agent, that there was something fundamentally wrong with the world. My outlook for mankind was a pessimistic one since I believed man to be responsible for his own state.

This summer I have had the occasion to come even closer to these men since I took the job of shipping clerk (who was on his vacation) under whom these men work.

Their ideas are just as anyone's when it comes to morals, but a certain hopelessness runs thru their make-up caused by their initial setback which deadens their conscience and kills their sense of duty to it.

They were born amidst the same surroundings in which they now live (heredity) and they were raised in these surroundings (environment). They married women who were raised the same they were and the final result is not a marriage but sort of a mutual consent to stand for the other if little obligations are filled. About the big aspect of marriage they seem to care little. They have a family, but each has his own means of pleasure on the side.

If these men could be made to see that there is a bit of lost motion in this supposedly rigid machine called heredity and environment and that their hope lies in an exercise of this lost motion, they could save themselves and their offspring much misery. It seems, however, a part of environment to keep them from seeing this and again we are back where we started, heredity and environment.

If the above seems too much removed from what you wanted, you will pardon me, I hope, since a person always becomes enthusiastic about his own views.

A clerical worker became interested in Hardy thru a University extension course and writes:

Most of Thomas Hardy's novels contain the spirit of fatalism. I do not know if that was his own opinion of life, but as a rule a man's personal convictions are reflected in his writings, so I assume that Hardy was a fatalist.

He held that regardless of what man is or does his fate is predestined. A man is born into this world thru no wish of his own, and of parents and under conditions over which he has no control. Later, he may have certain plans and ambitions, but these are not realized if the fates have decided otherwise. Humanity is as a wingless fly on a desk. The fly is put on the desk against its own wish. Then it crawls in one direction, and the pencil stops it and makes it go in a different direction. It climbs up a ruler, but the pencil pushes it down. It hops over the pencil point, if the pencil wishes it to. It tries in vain to jump over the edge of the desk out of reach of the pencil. Finally, when the pencil is tired of playing it will lead the fly to the brink of the ink-well and push it in. In this way the pencil of fate plays with the flies of humanity.

I do not claim to be a fatalist, but much in life is as Hardy pictures it. Two men may start out in life equally equipped and with the same opportunities and ambitions. Both will work equally as hard. The one will get the breaks and get somewhere, while the other gets the accidents and is a failure. If we do not have these experiences, we at least know of people who have. Hardy's tragedies are so interesting because they are true to life.

The views on Hardy of a student in a Negro high school are interesting:

While in school this past semester we made a study of the Victorian poets and novelists. We were given an opportunity to select a writer and to discuss his life and works. About this time I happened to read an article in the *Literary Digest* entitled "Thomas Hardy, Last of the Victorians." This account was so interesting that I decided to read some of his works. Probably the thing that interested me most was his interest in nature and the common people.

I have read *Tess of the D'Urbervilles, Far From the Madding Crowd, The Return of the Native,* and *Jude the Obscure.*

I liked *Tess of the D'Urbervilles* best. In this book we are given such accurate descriptions of birds, land, crops and geological information. Then, too, his philosophy of life "that man is least important and is a creature of fate" is brought out very clearly.

I, like Hardy, believe that man is least important and that nature is all supreme.

The last is from a seamstress:

I became interested in Hardy's work because a dear friend whose literary taste I admire recommended *Jude the Obscure* to me.

Since then I have read and greatly enjoyed *A Pair of Blue Eyes, The Return of the Native, Tess of the D'Urbervilles,* and *Under the Greenwood Tree.*

Of all these, I like *Jude the Obscure* because I felt so sorry for poor Jude who, strive as he will to advance himself, is always held down by circumstances that prove that his life is unsuccessful and ill-fated. Hardy is so sympathetic and offers no excuses for Jude's ignominious failure—it is just fate.

Yes, my philosophy of life agrees with his as I understand Hardy's philosophy in the books which I've read. He accepts life as it is, offers no solutions to its problems, but makes one feel, with his marvelous descriptional ability, a deep bond of sympathy for his fellow-man. I enjoy Hardy's poetry, too.

The most striking thing in the letters I received, including the ones quoted, is that those who wrote them in most part accept the "intractability of circum-

stances" as Hardy expresses it, that intractability of
circumstances affecting irretrievably human beings
like Tess and Jude and Michael Henchard.   These
readers agree with Hardy that happiness is "but the
occasional episode in a general drama of pain."   To
men who hold such a point of view unbearable
Hardy says:

> "O sweet sincerity!—
> Where modern methods be
> Where scope for thine and thee?
>
> "Life may be sad past saying,
> Its greens for ever graying,
> Its faiths to dust decaying;
>
> "And youth may have foreknown it,
> And riper seasons shown it,
> But custom cries: 'Disown it:
>
> " 'Say ye rejoice, though grieving,
> Believe, while unbelieving,
> Behold, without perceiving!'
>
> "—Yet, would men look at true things,
> And unilluded view things,
> And count to bear undue things,
>
> "The real might mend the seeming,
> Facts better their foredeeming,
> And Life its disesteeming."

WHO READS CARL SANDBURG?

Fifteen years ago the critics had their fling at Sandburg. Today he is accepted. Anthologies of modern verse include him—some with due praise, others without enthusiasm. What about the general reader, the gentle reader, the man in the street, the flapper, flaming youth? Are they reading him? Where will you find them, that we may ask them? They are all represented among the users of the modern public library, today the most democratic, and as yet the freest and least restrained agency in placing the fruits of knowledge (the good and the evil, shall we say), before the people. It is for them to choose—the detective story for the tired business man, the good sweet story for the good sweet woman, but Sandburg for others.

An examination of the records in the public library of a large American city disclosed the identity of about one hundred recent readers of Sandburg's poetry. They in most part have the same street addresses as the characters of Sandburg's own creation. Today everything is measured from the electron to the universe, but who has attempted to measure that elusive and yet certain influence of one personality upon another? We have not even begun to think about the possibility of the measurement of the effect of an author upon his reader. Yet nothing is more certain than that an author read and appropriated with enthusiasm may change the very fabric of the soul of the reader.

The impact of a Sandburg upon the thoughts, the emotions, the feelings, cannot as yet be measured, but it can be taken account of in one's imagination —it can at least be shot at in the dark. As we bring forward some of these hundred readers from the common walks of life, but with something from the neck up worth possessing, perhaps we can sense the effect of a Sandburg upon the stenographer, the typist, the police clerk and the reporter by lines from his writings, taken at random, which seem to speak directly to them.

To the stenographer: "By day the skyscraper looms in the sun and has a soul. . . . It is the men and women, boys and girls, so poured in and out all day, that give the building a soul of dreams and thoughts and memories."

To the typist: "Smiles and tears of each office girl go into the soul of the building, just the same as the master-men who rule the building."

To the Negro reader: "I am the nigger. Singer of songs, Dancer. . . . Softer than fluff of cotton. . . . Harder than dark earth Roads beaten in the sun By the bare feet of slaves."

To the minister: "Lay me on an anvil, O God. Beat me and hammer me into a crowbar. Let me pry loose old walls. Let me lift and loosen old foundations."

To the newspaper reporter: "Speak softly—the sacred cows may hear. Speak easy—the sacred cows must be fed."

To the police clerk: "Out of the whirling womb
of time come millions of men and their feet crowd
the earth and they cut one another's throats for
room to stand and among them all are not two thumbs
alike."

To the musician: "A man saw the whole world
as a grinning skull and cross bones. . . . Then he went
to a Mischa Elman concert. . . . Music washed something or other inside of him. Music broke down and
rebuilt something or other in his head and heart. . . .
He was the same man in the same world as before.
Only there was a singing fire and a climb of roses
everlastingly over the world he looked on."

To the waitress: "Shake back your hair, O red-
headed girl. Let go your laughter and keep your
two proud freckles on your chin."

To the manager of a beauty parlor: "The woman
named Tomorrow sits with a hairpin in her teeth
and takes her time and does her hair in the way she
wants it and fastens at last the last braid and coil and
puts the hairpin where it belongs and turns and
drawls: Well, what of it? My grandmother, Yester-
day, is gone. What of it? Let the dead be dead."

To the book agent: "This is a good book? Yes?
Throw it at the moon—Let her go—Spang—This
book for the moon. . . Yes? And then—other books,
good books, even the best books—shoot 'em with a
long twist at the moon—Yes?"

To the man who puts himself down a laborer:
"Men who sunk the pilings and mixed the mortar are
laid in graves where the wind whistles a wild song
without words."

Among others of the hundred readers to whom
he does not speak so directly, are many high school
and college students, a few grade school children, a
good representation of teachers, a department store
saleswoman, two advertising men, a mechanic, a
printer, a shoe salesman, a physician and the wife of
another physician, several who designate themselves
as clerks, and the wives of men engaged in similar
occupations. The list is as significant in the vocations
which are found unrepresented.   There is not a
lawyer on the list. "Why does a hearse horse snicker,
hauling a lawyer away?" There are only one physician and two ministers.   There is only one business
man and I happen to know that he calls his vocation
merely a meal ticket—his avocation being that of a
playwright. It is interesting to observe that a similar
recent study of readers of William James indicated
that much the same classes of people were reading
him as read Sandburg. Perhaps I cannot prove the
fact, but I would be willing to wager that on the list
of Sandburg readers there are not many "go-getters"
—100 per cent Americans and 20th century "he-men,"
which words in themselves are sufficient to make most
of us swell with over-weaning pride.

In order to find out what these readers thought
of Sandburg's poetry, I wrote to some of them, asking them to tell me how they happened to become
interested in his poetry; whether they liked or disliked
it; did they consider it poetry, and would it live, and
what poems did they especially like or dislike? Most
of the answers, which in some cases were very full,
showed an understanding of Sandburg which in their

estimate of his place in present day American literature corresponds rather closely with the varying
estimate of the literary critics who have written about
him. Here are some extracts from these letters:

A minister writes:

First of all I should like to say that I found the
Chicago poems very interesting and powerful. The
latter attribute is the most commendable in any of the
works of Sandburg I believe. You ask me if I consider his works poetry and I say without hesitation and
very dogmatically "no." The most fitting definition
of poetry in my estimation is one that I found in a
book on German literature which translated would be,
"Poetry is beautiful thought in beautiful form." Some
of his things when weighed in the balance are woefully
lacking in beautiful thought or form and all of them
lack one or the other. His works may live as a sample
of the product of this age but never for their literary
value, is my belief.

"I have seen your painted women standing under the
lamp-posts luring the innocent country boys,"—he gives
us a cross section of life written in powerful prose. That
is all we can claim for him.

A janitor in a store drops a word of disparage-
ment as to Sandburg, but calls attention to his own
poetry, samples of which he sent me. He says:

i am quite a greate reader But have not read Sand-
burgs poems very much for i did not cair much for
them so i can not say much about them.

i am a poet myself or think i am aneyhow. i com-
menced writing Poetry when i was eight years old. i
am almost 65 now. Will send you a few samples of
my Poor work on that line and you may Be able to

do something for me and if you cant their is no harm done. i can write poor poetry, But make my living by hard work.

A teacher in the public schools of St. Louis expresses her appreciation as follows:

I became interested in Sandburg's poetry thru a literature course which a roommate at University of Chicago took; and the subsequent reading and discussions of Sandburg's poetry. We often read his Chicago Poems aloud to each other.

Yes, I like his poems, because of his understanding and feeling for life—the expression of thoughts which I have had but could not adequately express. His feelings for the poorer classes of Chicago masses, etc., etc.

In recalling his poems I find that I remember his vivid word pictures, so that his poems are called to mind by the mental visual image the poem made. The uniqueness of form and style are also attractive.

Is it poetry? Yes—and no. Poetry when we consider the beauty of idea and ease of expression, but not poetry if we shall limit ourselves to narrow meter forms, rhyming, etc.

If any of the modern poetry lives (which I think it will), Sandburg's and Teasdale's will always be much read and appreciated.

I am especially fond of "Lines to a Contemporary Bunk-Shooter." The first time I read it I hated it, but later grew to appreciate it for its frankness, vividness, and life.

The following comes from the pen of a fourteen-year old high school student:

Am answering your unusual request because I, like all poor mortals, love to give an opinion, and because I love to write—anything.

I became interested in Sandburg's poetry only after having been obliged by duty to read some modern poet's works. I chose Sandburg's because I had never before read any of them, tho I had heard something of the promising author. You may be interested to know that out of a third term English class of forty students, only one chose to read Sandburg.

I am very fond of Carl Sandburg's work at times, tho at other times they seem exceedingly hard to become interested in. I believe, tho, that one never enjoys the same thing always, so, on the whole, I do love his poetry—very much. The reasons for my liking it, are, for the most part unknown to me, tho I suppose its main appeal to me is in that it is so very—different. Then, too, I, with Sandburg, love, admire, and am inspired by the wheat fields of Illinois. Sandburg's is the best description of them I have ever read. Also, my dream city is Chicago. Oh, Sandburg seems to get at the heart of his themes with an astonishing agility.

Most certainly I consider it poetry for it is indeed "the best words in the best way." What else could it be but poetry, for it seems to sing, and makes something respond and sing within the reader, too.

As I am not a prophetess at all, I can scarcely say whether or not his poetry will live. Or perhaps I should say, it shall live—in me, tho I doubt if it will live in the hearts of the people, as did the works of Longfellow and the other more conservative poets. On the other hand, Poe was not at all conservative, and his poetry is immortal (especially the beautiful Annabel Lee). My poor opinions are as nothing. I cannot say.

It has been such a very long time since I read *Corn Huskers* that I cannot remember any titles. I am sure that the poems dealing with the "sun on the wheat fields" were my especial favorites. However (you have aroused my interest in Carl Sandburg again, you see!) I intend to read *Corn Huskers* once more and procure from the

public library others of his works, and then, if you
wish, I shall mail you the names of my favorites, and the
ones I care least for.

P.S. These are only the opinions of a fourteen-year-
old girl, so do not be annoyed at my style of writing
and expression of my opinions. My name is at your
service, if you wish.

Another teacher writes in part:

Just by way of wanting to know something about
Modern American Poets, I took, several years ago, an
evening course at Washington University from Professor
Jones. I found the course extremely interesting and
found that my professor was particularly interested in
Carl Sandburg's poetry. It is perhaps because of Pro-
fessor Jones' interest that I found myself very fond of
Carl Sandburg's verse.

I wish that I were home at present and could get
at some of my notes. At present I am attending
Columbia University, and am quite busy with mid-term
exams. If such were not the case, I should enjoy reading
over many of Sandburg's poems and should enjoy giving
you my impressions.

Not being a poetic scholar, I cannot express myself
in the language of poets. I believe that his is poetry; of
course, his style is very free but that does not make
his product any the less poetry. I love the feeling, the
sound, the music that comes to me as I read his "Cool
Tombs" and "Grass." Those are the two poems that
come to my mind as I write.

An advertising man for a manufacturing concern
writes at length of himself and his unflattering views
of Sandburg, which are quoted here in part:

I am an amateur scribbler with a keen realization of
my own limitations but an equally keen enjoyment of
an occasional spree in the realm of literary self expression. Like most amateurs of whatever degree of

promise, I am afflicted with friends and relatives who persist in regarding me as a potential second Shakespeare. It was in an effort to convince them—a successful effort, by the way—that I was not destined to cast any light on the literary heavens, that led up to my acquaintance with the redoutable Mr. Sandburg.

I cannot say that I either liked or disliked the works of this strange writer. I will confess to an occasional flash of admiration as he created some extremely vivid image, but on the whole, I read his poems with a feeling of tolerant amusement.

I do not consider myself an absolute reactionary, by any means. I read the works of Masefield, Noyes and Lindsay with the utmost enjoyment. Most of Amy Lowell's work—even her free verse, I found enjoyable. Sandburg, however, I found merely grotesque, for the most part.

I may be wrong,—I probably am—but it seems to me that the reason Whitman's works will continue to live is that he plunged deep down into the crucible of life and brought up the pure molten metal. Sandburg, on the contrary, seems to me to have skimmed off the slag.

If you have ever been near a huge steel mill, you will appreciate the above figure of speech. When the slag is dumped, there is a tremendous splash and flying of sparks, but when it has cooled, there is only an ugly shapeless mass. Pure metal, however, runs to the rolling mill and is worked into enduring articles of commerce and enjoys (if one may use that term) a certain sort of immortality analogous to that enjoyed by the works of a true literary genius.

It has been some time since I read any of Mr. Sandburg's works and I cannot recall a single one of them, which made a sufficiently deep impression on me, so that I could say that I either liked or disliked any single bit of his work. My whole feeling toward this man's writings may be caused by conflicting temperament; it probably is. So far as that is concerned, however, if others who comply with your request would be equally frank, you would probably find that they would have to make the same confession, if, by any chance, they had the slightest understanding of the reason for whatever reactions they may have.

I think that one reason why critics are usually treated in such a contemptuous manner, is the fact that so much criticism is based on personal feeling or on a little understood reaction of temperament. After all, what standards have we to guide us in criticising the works of such men as Sandburg?

They are pioneers. Recognizing the fact that poetry, the last thing in the world which ought to be standard-ized, was rapidly declining into a state where poetry, so-called, would be produced after the same fashion as Ford cars, they went to the extreme limit of revolt.

Not all of them went so far as Mr. Sandburg, Lowell and the freak followers of our friend Harriet Monroe in Chicago. Many reached the truly sublime heights. I think that future generations will so regard Masefield, Noyes and to some extent, Frost, Lindsay and Robinson.

As for the utter extremists—and I regard Sand-burg as falling in that category—it is my opinion— merely an opinion—they will be lumped together in the consideration of future critics as being collectively responsible for the new literary movement, that their names may live in that connection, but that very little of what they have produced will survive any other way than as literary curiosities produced in an era of transition.

The wife of a man, who in the city directory is classified as a clerk, writes appreciatively of Sand-burg:

I first became interested in modern poetry when I took a course in "contemporary poetry" at Washington

University. Here I read a few of Sandburg's poems for the first time. I liked some of them so well I have since read all his works.

I cannot say I like all his poetry but I like some of it. It seems to me that some of it is rather crude and lacks the finish associated with any art. I do not like the strident element in his poetry. Sandburg's object is to give us his impression of life and since some life is crude and strident Sandburg accomplishes what he wishes to do. I admire the technique he employs but do not like what he produces. It seems to me that at times he shows a lack of judgment in his selection of subject matter.

But in many of his poems we have expressions of great beauty and perfect construction and unity. Most of his figures of speech are unique and striking, and if not too prosaic, are pleasing. The most pronounced note in his better poems is his tender sympathy and understanding of all kinds of life and his resignation to a hopeless death as portrayed in his philosophy of living.

It depends on one's standard for poetry whether or not one can say Sandburg does or does not write it. According to my standard of poetry Sandburg writes poetry. He also writes many poems that are not poetry.

I think Sandburg's most beautiful poems will live because of the merit they have. But we are living in a transitional period of poetry and Sandburg, I believe, is the greatest of this period. For that reason, if not for the merit of his poetry, the best of his work will be preserved.

I like the "Undertow," "Cool Tombs," "The Harbor," "Lost," "The Nurse-Mother," "Joy," and his other poems of like nature. I cannot say I really dislike any of his poems but I do not care for "Chicago." No doubt Sandburg in this poem does exactly what he attempts to do but I do not care for that type of poetry. "Cornhuskers" and "Smoke and Steel" are better, but I do not care for them as I do for his shorter, tenderer

poems. Sandburg can be infinitely tender and understanding and his poems in this mood are his best. It
seems to me that these are the poems that cause him to
rank very high as a poet today.

The wife of the manager of a motor company
says she first had her attention called to Sandburg
when her pastor quoted from the *Fish Monger*. She
writes:

There is, of course, truth in what he says, and from
what little I know of his poems, it is well put. You ask
if I consider it poetry. In Webster's Dictionary the
definition of Poetry is: "The embodiment in appropriate
rhythmical language, usually metrical, of beautiful or
high thoughts, imagination, or emotion." Many of his
things surely are not that but they do stir one to better
conditions, just as Dickens's descriptions do, and they
do paint portions of Chicago in vivid raw colors.

The only letter completely condemning Sandburg
came anonymously and reads as follows:

I dislike the poetry of Sandburg because its effects
are not esthetic in any degree.

I do not consider it poetry. It lacks the beauty of
expression and thought that characterizes real poetry.

It is doubtful that Sandburg's poetry will live, for
it is not sufficiently distinctive; it is merely a part of
the mass of so-called modern verse.

I consider Sandburg's poetry vulgar, at times; coarse,
brutal, materialistic and sordid. To one who has been
held breathless by the musical cadence, the magic
imagery, the wealth of word and thought of Shelley and
Keats, or any of the real poets, the so-called poetry of
Sandburg is as a transition from the sublime to the
ridiculous. Slang will never be the medium of poetic
expression. The golden chain of poetic thought is

roughly torn asunder when a slang or exceedingly commonplace phrase is introduced. No, Sandburg may have been a good newspaper man; he could, perhaps, have written essays; but he was no poet. To call his work poetry is a sacrilege to the muse, a desecration of the name of poesy.

Two letters deal especially with Sandburg's *Abraham Lincoln—The Prairie Years.* One is from a teacher of evident literary appreciation. She says in part:

I have read Carl Sandburg's *Abraham Lincoln*; his poems, one or two volumes, some of the Rootabaga Stories; have heard him speak, read his verse and thump his banjo. I like him, the funny stories, the shorter poems and the Lincoln. I was charmed, too, with the man himself.

I first liked Lincoln better after I saw Drinkwater's play; then after I read Sandburg, liked the human touch —I mean one's feeling that he was so humanly humorous or is it the reverse, so humorously human. It has been a long time since I read the book and many things are between then and now. I remember I liked it and stayed up because interested, as well as to do up a two-volume set to get it back to the library. My aunt, too, read it and altho a very Southern person with traditional prejudices, liked Lincoln better and enjoyed the book.

A man I was talking with the other day who reads considerably, travels (in Europe twice), is a college man of years ago, however, not literary especially, had not heard of Sandburg.

I introduced Sandburg into a literary class last year in a State Teachers College. Except one or two, they had not read any of him; most of them did not know he existed. Kipling and Neihardt were about the only modern poets they knew. They liked Sandburg, especially the men.

The other is from a police clerk:

In reply to your letter asking for my opinion of Carl Sandburg's *Abraham Lincoln, the Prairie Years,* wish to say that it is one of many books that I shall always be glad that I have had the pleasure to read and enjoy.

I ran across some of Mr. Carl Sandburg's poetry some years ago. I enjoyed it so much that I read everything of Sandburg's that I could find. Later I heard of his new monumental work, *Abraham Lincoln.* I procured it quickly and enjoyed reading every line of it. Ordinarily I find the reading of biographies dull, they are usually smoothed over, white washed here and there, done so I guess because the truth is never fit for publication, but here is one in a different style and purpose, done neatly, clearly and poetically. There are whole pages in it that read like poetry. The description of Lincoln plodding thru mud and muck of Illinois country roads is a treat and as real to me as the day I myself plowed thru it.

I like reading it because I found it instructive, entertaining and not a page to be dull. I believe Sandburg has painted Lincoln as he really was—a great big giant, come up out of the wilderness and the hinderland with great big broad shoulders and bared chest to strike a new note in the history of his country.

To my mind Sandburg's Lincoln will ring round the world as a work of greatness, for whosoever reads it will come to know Lincoln as no other man has written of him.

I wonder whether the fourteen-year-old girl has not answered the question as to whether Sandburg's poetry will live when she says, "It will live in me," and again the question as to whether it is poetry when she says, "What else could it be but poetry, for it seems to sing and make something sing in the reader, too." I have asked myself the same questions that I put to those whose letters appear here and the answers I give are like theirs, uncontaminated by any knowledge of the technique of poetry. To be sure I have read books on poetry and have enjoyed them, especially Max Eastman's *Enjoyment of Poetry*, but I know not a whit more about how poetry is made on that account, altho they have added to my appreciation of poetry. But there is one thing I do know, and that is the effect poetry has on me. If I were to attempt to define poetry, I would say that it was that form of literary expression which in the fewest words can affect man most profoundly. That satisfies me, for it allows me to consider both Keats and Sandburg as poets.

Sandburg's poetry is not like that of Shelley or Keats, yet it stirs my emotions, not the same emotions as does Shelley's *Ode to the Skylark* or Keats' *Autumn*, but just as deeply—perhaps more deeply. More deeply, because Sandburg's poetry goes down deep into the life of this twentieth century of which he is a part—of which I am a part. It is a life I understand. At those ugly things in life at which he rebels—at those things I rebel. Of all the poets I know, not excepting Walt Whitman, Sandburg is not excelled in his sympathy with the common and even the lowest of humanity, with the great unwashed, with the boobs and the flappers, with the 75 per cent of our population whom the intelligence testers set down as morons. Sandburg understands them all. He interprets them and draws from them the beauty hidden away in the dark recesses of their outwardly unlovely exteriors.

Will Sandburg's poetry live? I am willing to abide by the answer of the fourteen-year-old girl. It will live in me and from the letters which I have quoted I know that there are other "me's" beside my own, in whom Sandburg's poetry is now living, and I believe that in the years to come there will be still other "me's" yet unborn in whom Carl Sandburg will live and will stir still pools in the hidden places of their souls.

Sandburg in his language limits himself to the Middle West, but in his love for mankind he circles the globe; in his philosophy he searches the heights in man's life and penetrates the depths in man's death. "At a Window" he looks out upon life and says:

Give me hunger,
O you Gods that sit and give
The world its orders.
Give me hunger, pain and want,
Shut me out with shame and failure
From your doors of gold and fame,
Give me your shabbiest, weariest hunger!

But leave me a little love,
A voice to speak to me in the day end,
A hand to touch me in the dark room
Breaking the long loneliness.
In the dusk of day-shapes
Blurring the sunset,

One little wandering, western star
Thrust out from the changing shores of shadow.
Let me go to the window,
Watch there the day-shapes of dusk
And wait and know the coming
Of a little love.

WHO READS BERNARD SHAW?

Hello G. B. S.:

I am addressing you in this familiar manner because it is the way you addressed me and other Americans in a recent radio talk when your voice boomed out in resonant tones "Hello, America!"

A dramatist can tell something about his audience by attending a play—what effects he secures, what characters make hits, what quips get over—but what does the dramatist know about his readers except that his published plays sell in more or less quantity? I decided recently to find out something about your readers and so examined the reading of 431 of them, as shown by the records of the St. Louis Public Library. These are only a small part of your readers in St. Louis, but a sufficient number to make a real cross-section. They may be considered typical Americans, for St. Louis is a typical American city. In addition to learning what I could from the records of the library I wrote to some of your readers and they responded with their opinions of your plays and yourself.

In identifying these 431 readers, I was interested to note that a complete society, with all or nearly all of the essential and non-essential industries and occupations, could be supplied. So I propose that we take them to an uninhabited island and set up a

Shaw colony. I am writing this letter to you to ask you to join the colony to be established in your honor. The island is located in the Mississippi River. You will find it easily because we expect to use your own best methods of bally-hoo to attract attention. I shall now proceed to tell you more about the colonists.

In any colony, one of the first requirements would be to provide housing. Among your 431 readers are men equipped to take care of this need in all respects. There are three real estate agents, one a Negro, and the wives of two other real estate agents. My record does not show whether they have read *Widowers' Houses,* in which you give your idea of a real estate owner or landlord. An architect had read six of your plays but not *Mrs. Warren's Profession,* in which Praed, the architect, appears. There is also an architect's wife, who says:

I was first introduced to Shaw in a modern English Literature course at the University of Illinois.

Since "school-days" I have read for my own enlightenment and entertainment *Man and Superman, Major Barbara, Candida,* and *The Apple Cart.* I saw *The Apple Cart* when it was here.

I admire Shaw's clever diction and provocative conversation, and I like to "chuckle" with him over "things as they are," but I do rather dislike taking part in his somewhat morbid outlook for civilization in general. Somehow I cannot take seriously his paradoxes on America and Russia. I feel that his attitude toward America is "assumed" to a certain extent. It is irritating to be called irresponsible, avaricious, and perdition-bent, but I can even then take Shaw "with all his faults and like him just the same."

I like *Candida* very much, but I enjoyed reading *The Apple Cart* even more because of its political application.

After the land has been bought from one of the real estate men and the plan has been made for the house by the architect, then a carpenter will be needed, and there is one who recently has been reading *Fanny's First Play* in German. For those who prefer a house built of brick there is an excellent bricklayer to be recommended, and I am sure you will not question that he is a good bricklayer after reading what he says about you:

You see I'm a bricklayer and our work is never very steady. I formed the habit of reading to kill time when out of work. Of course, we used the library, a friend and myself. Went almost every week. Bad habit. If all the books I've read were placed end to end they'd reach something.

I don't suppose you'd approve of my slipshod way of reading. Nothing serious about it. A book I read and like is forgotten in a little while, but the author I remember. So I can try him again some time. That's how it is with Shaw.

I became interested from reading references to him and his plays in different magazine articles and to satisfy my curiosity started to read Shaw. Something about his way of asserting himself happened to appeal to me and I proceeded to read out that section of the library, whenever I felt like Shaw.

I seldom go to theatres so I've never seen one of his plays, and as for being able to say what I like or don't like, I simply don't remember. Taking what I've read as one lump, it goes over with a bang. I like it.

About the man Shaw. My opinion isn't worth anything at all. I don't agree with his criticisms but I certainly don't resent them either. He interests and amuses me. I heard him broadcast sometime ago and I'm sure I like him.

I am sorry that this bricklayer did not comment on the bricklayer in *Man and Superman* and the bricklayer's wife who spent all her seventeen pounds on her husband's funeral and then went to the workhouse with her seven children.

To the building group may be added an interior decorator, who has been reading recently the *Intelligent Woman's Guide to Socialism,* and the wife of a cabinet maker, who has been indulging in *Getting Married.* A fire insurance agent, among the readers, is present to insure houses of the Shaw colony.

It is essential to have someone to feed this community of Shaw readers, so there is a grocer who has been reading the *Quintessence of Ibsenism,* and there is a confectioner who has been reading *Back to Methuselah.* A short letter leaves to the imagination what he really thinks of you:

In answer to your letter requesting my opinion of Bernard Shaw and his works, I wish to state that it has been my experience that a magazine, newspaper, or other periodical is nothing more than an organ of education or miseducation, depending upon the political, social, or economic leanings of its backers. Therefore, my opinion would be useless, and I believe no publication but a radical one would consent to publish what I think of Bernard Shaw.

A Negro housekeeper, who is a widow and a reader of *Saint Joan,* is the only one of the 431 readers doing domestic service for pay.

The health of this colony of Shaw readers should
be well taken care of, as there are fourteen represented
in the group who minister to the physical welfare
of the community: two druggists, one having read
Caesar and Cleopatra and the other the *Intelligent
Woman's Guide to Socialism.* In spite of your
diatribes against doctors, they evidently are reading
you, as four are represented here—more than most
other professional groups. It does not happen, however, that the library records show they have read
The Doctor's Dilemma or the *Philanderer,* in which
you drop your most destructive bombs on their profession. There are two nurses, one of whom has
read *The Doctor's Dilemma,* and a dentist, who has
read *Major Barbara.* Let us hope that he has made
the acquaintance of the dentist, Valentine, in *You
Never Can Tell.* There is even a foot specialist, who
has been reading *Caesar and Cleopatra,* and a dieti-
cian, who has been reading *Androcles and the Lion.*

Provision is made also for the domestic animals,
the horses, the cats and the dogs, in the colony, for
there is a veterinarian who has read *John Bull's
Other Island* and *Major Barbara.* There are in this
health group several others employed in various
capacities in hospitals.

In this Shaw colony I suppose we must have
some kind of a government, and those to carry it on
are not lacking. At least there are the wives of two
policemen, who the records show read a number of
your plays. The strong arm methods displayed in
Androcles and the Lion, as well as the Sheriff in
Shewing up of Blanco Posnet, might well be interest-

ing to both policemen and their wives. There are
five lawyers who have read many of your plays, but
not as far as I know *Captain Brassbound's Conver-*
sion, in which they might have seen how a judge, in
the person of Sir Howard Hallam, was wrapped
around a woman's finger, or *You Never Can Tell*,
where they might have met that resourceful attorney
Bohun and his more resourceful father, a hotel waiter.

In this group of readers also there are a court
officer, a court reporter, a city inspector, a letter
carrier, a post office clerk, and a post office messenger.
The latter had much to say about you which I shall
quote in part only:

I do not know where or how I became interested in
Shaw's writings. I have never seen any of his plays.
Perhaps it was thru the newspapers who have always
featured him in pictures or articles. I have read *The*
Doctor's Dilemma, Saint Joan, Getting Married, and *Man*
and Superman. I liked *Doctor's Dilemma* best.

Man and Superman I think is too idealistic. The
Utopia that he breathes in this story is all dispelled
when one awakens to the realities of life, the futile wars,
the political maneuverings, the prejudices of races,
individualistic tendencies, ignorance regarding eugenics.
Superman is a remote object and hope of humanity.

Shaw is vituperative in the preface of his plays.
I think he is sincere in his convictions. He is hard, I'll
admit, with an inclination to expose the pretentions of
those that he thinks take undue assumptions, as doctors,
lawyers, politicians, clergymen, and writers. Shaw up-
sets accepted beliefs. Shaw makes you think, because
he thinks for you. I believe his attitude towards America
is sincere. Why should we care what he thinks of this
country? I can't understand his socialistic tendencies,
his own life and living contradicts his preaching. Shaw

is contradictory, still if he shows us both sides of a problem we can judge for ourselves, so thanks to him. All in all I admire Shaw. I think he is great. I like his personality.

Among your readers are a sufficient number to provide wearing apparel: a dressmaker, a seamstress, two milliners, a costumer, the wives of two dry-cleaners, and a tailor. Let us hope that the latter has made the acquaintance of Androcles, a Christian tailor, and the lion who did not forget a kindly act. A designer knows Androcles and many of your other characters. She says:

About fifteen years ago I became interested in Shaw's writings by reading *Androcles and the Lion.* I have read his *Pygmalion, Man and Superman, Major Barbara, Saint Joan,* and *Ellen Terry and Bernard Shaw; a correspondence. Pygmalion* is the only play of Shaw's that I have seen on the stage. It seems unnecessary to say that I believe *Saint Joan* to be Shaw's greatest and one of the finest pieces of literature in our language. I also consider *Major Barbara* a great play and especially fine as a study of the contrast between the progressive and the conservative points of view.

I cannot judge Shaw as a man except from his writing, but I believe him to be a sincere worker for the betterment of humanity, as well as a great writer. That he finds it necessary in the course of his work to dramatize himself is no discredit to him. Wasn't it Voltaire who said that every great man must be something of a charlatan in order that the world may hear of his greatness? The world would be better off if we had more "charlatans" of his type. I heartily disagree with his political views and feel that he is not particularly well qualified to pass judgment on economics but see no reason for the antagonism which many people feel

on that score. As for his criticism of America, where is
our sense of humor? I consider Shaw a fearless
crusader as well as a matchless writer, and that he is
one of the great minds of our time.

Factory workers among your readers should fill
a useful place in the new Shaw colony: a man and a
woman, workers in a shoe factory, a furniture worker,
a finisher in a garment company, a packer, a worker
in a hat factory, a drill press operator, an inspector
in a steel works, a worker in a can company. Nearly
all of them read *Major Barbara* and so met among
its characters Bill Walker, "a rough customer," and
Bilton, the factory foreman, as well as Undershaft,
the explosives manufacturer.

Among the readers also may be mentioned manu-
facturers and executives that include a manager of
a hat factory, who has been reading *Back to
Methuselah*, a serum manufacturer, a reader of the
Intelligent Woman's Guide to Socialism, a president
of a neckwear company, reader of *Heartbreak House*,
the wife of the president of a woolen company, a
reader of *Major Barbara*, and the wife of an execu-
tive in a petroleum company.

The industrial development of the Shaw colony
is assured, for men who work with machinery, from
the engineer to the plain mechanic, are represented
among your readers. There are three draftsmen,
all readers of *Androcles and the Lion*, a construction
engineer, the wife of an electrical engineer, three
engineers of industrial plants, a structural engineer,
two machinists, a mechanic and two mechanics' wives,

a pipe-fitter's wife, and two chemists. A chemical engineering student thus expresses himself:

I regard Shaw as one of the best authors and most intelligent men in the world today. As a result of reading *The Doctor's Dilemma,* I continued until I have read practically all his plays, two of his novels, and his *Woman's Guide to Socialism.* In all his plays and other writings I have found none which was not immensely interesting, and it is often a question as to which is the more interesting, the play or the preface. His *Guide* is probably his best, as it summarizes his whole thought in one volume. I do not see how anyone can disagree with his indictment of present conditions; the only cause for argument is the remedy. As for his critical attitude toward this country, he is perfectly justified. However, as he has kindly shown us, the people of his own country are just as foolish.

There will certainly be a sufficient number of the white-collared clerical human machines in the colony of Shaw readers. Except for students and teachers, they are the largest class. There are twenty-seven stenographers and secretaries whose reading embraces nearly all of your plays, with *Androcles and the Lion* in the ascendancy. One of them, who became interested from amateur dramatic presentations and who has read *Androcles and the Lion, St. Joan, Major Barbara,* and *The Apple Cart,* says:

I am interested in Shaw's criticisms, but think his plays too preachy, therefore undramatic and lengthy soliloquies. I feel that Shaw is overwhelmed by the problems he attacks and consequently fears to attack them in a straightforward manner, but reverts to satire. I do enjoy reading him.

There are also two dictaphone operators and
six typists, one of whom at least has read *Candida*,
and knows Proserpine Garnett, the brisk little typist
of Reverend James Mavor Morell.

Bookkeepers and accountants number fourteen,
office boys two, and time keeper one. Of clerks
there are twenty-eight, among whom a railroad clerk,
who says he is 26 years old, a high school graduate
and pretty much of a reader, comments thus:

A friend of mine had been reading Shaw, and urged
that I do likewise. Previous to this I had very seldom
read plays, confining my reading mostly to biography,
history, novels and periodicals. I have read *Saint Joan,
Man and Superman*, and *Caesar and Cleopatra*, having
had a minor part in *Androcles and the Lion* when pre-
sented by an amateur theatrical group. *Man and Superman* and *Androcles and the Lion* were the two that I
liked best, of the plays I have read so far. In these
Shaw is witty and clever at poking fun at human short-
comings. *St. Joan* I enjoyed, altho, it may be, he pre-
sented only one side of the story. *Caesar and Cleopatra*
struck me as being rather absurd; I could not imagine
Julius Caesar indulging in the frivolous conversation
carried on in the play, altho I have never made a deep
study of his character.

I thing Bernard Shaw is "all there." With his
criticism of the capitalistic system, with its senseless
striving and competition, resulting in wide-spread misery,
I whole-heartedly agree. His endorsement of Com-
munist Russia, after his visit there last year, particularly
pleased me; it showed that altho starting out as a
Fabian Socialist, his mind was not closed to new ideas.
Here is an author who is not blind to the spectacle of
the greatest social experiment ever undertaken.

A colony would need means of transportation and our Shaw readers are prepared to supply numerous ways of getting over the ground, including a street car conductor and a bus driver, both readers of *Androcles and the Lion*. It is to be expected that they have made the acquaintance of that inimitable chauffeur, Mr. Enry Straker, in *Man and Superman*. Others from this group of readers are a railroad fireman, a reader of *St. Joan*, several other railroad employes, and an airport engineer, kindred spirit, without doubt, of Joey Percival, the aviator in *Misalliance* who made a miraculous landing on a greenhouse.

Employes of the American Telephone Company for some reason evidently have a special liking for you, insuring the installation of an excellent telephone system in our colony. There are two young women telephone operators, one supervisor, two repairmen, several others with varied duties, and a telephone engineer who says:

I cannot definitely remember how I first became interested in Shaw's writings, tho I believe it was thru hearing older friends discuss his writings when a student in high school. While in college, an attempt of our dramatic club to produce one of Shaw's plays led to further interest. Finally, a more intelligent interest was prompted by seeing several of his plays on the professional stage.

My reading of Shaw has been confined entirely to the following plays: *Pygmalion, Androcles and the Lion, Man and Superman, Caesar and Cleopatra*, and *The Apple Cart*. On the professional stage I have seen *Pygmalion, Major Barbara, The Doctor's Dilemma*, and *The Apple Cart*. I read *Androcles and the Lion* and

Caesar and Cleopatra because I participated in a non-professional performance of these plays.

Shaw, as a man, irritates me with his conceit and cocksureness. He reminds me of a youngster who, tho he unquestionably may have possessed certain merits, has been so pampered by doting parents that he becomes obnoxious by his continuous and ostentatious display of talents. Were he a child, he should be taken on an old-fashioned trip to the woodshed and soundly spanked. He was undeniably clever (I used the past tense because I do not believe his latter work equals his former), but has now attained the unenviable status of a senile show-off.

As a dramatist, I do not suppose I can criticize him for using the stage to promulgate his social theories, since it is probably one of the surest methods of getting people to listen to you. Other dramatists, less capable than Shaw, have done and are still doing the same thing, but not, however, so consistently.

One cannot help but admire Shaw for his showmanship. This bewhiskered, golf-knickered satyr is the greatest showman since Barnum. He apparently delights in "pulling the leg" of the public—particularly the leg of the American public, for he is astute enough to know that tho the American public may resent his attitude it will nevertheless increase the sale of his books in this country—human nature is like that. If I could be convinced that I am correct in my suspicion that he often has his "tongue in his cheek," I could forgive him for ·much.

A young woman, who has read *Androcles and the Lion, Overruled* and *Pygmalion,* and characterizes herself as "nearly thirty years old, of Italian descent, telegrapher by trade and Catholic in religion," says:

I suppose that there is no question but that Shaw is a great playwright, but so many of his utterances seem so childish, that I find the question hard to decide whether the man is genius, or just a brilliant fool.

As for his "well-known critical attitude toward America," what isn't taken seriously can't be resented.

If your object is to preach your social gospel to teachers and students, the number of readers among them promises well for the Shaw colony. Teachers number eighteen white and two Negro; college students, seventy-seven white and three Negro; high school students, fifty-six white and three Negro; and grade school students, twenty. One of the teachers expresses her criticism thus:

I took a course on Modern Literature from Washington University and, of course, Shaw was one of the outstanding characters. I have never seen one of his plays on the stage. I read *The Man of Destiny, How He Lied to Her Husband, Man and Superman, Candida,* and *Back to Methuselah.* I can't say I like any of his books. I dislike *Back to Methuselah* most on account of his belittling the Bible. I like the position he takes on some questions, but just the opposite on others. For instance, he is a non-conformist, which is good in some things but not in others. There are a great many things in America today which need criticism, but not so radical as Shaw would do it. I think his criticism of America is absurd.

A college student, who has read Shaw's plays extensively, gives vent freely to his opinions:

I first became genuinely interested in Shaw's work thru reading Chesterton's work on him, tho I had met the plays before.

Read *Plays Pleasant and Unpleasant, Three Plays for Puritans, Major Barbara* and *John Bull's Other Island,*

Androcles, Pygmalion and *Overruled, Back to Methuselah, Man and Superman, Quintessence of Ibsenism,
Dramatic Opinions and Essays.* Saw *Man and Superman.* Best are: *Caesar and Cleopatra* (zenith of his
wit, less a piece of social propaganda than most), *Man
and Superman* (sustained brilliance). Least is *Widowers' Houses* (too obviously sermonistic, less witty).

Not quite the sincere altruist that Mr. Chesterton
and Mr. Henderson made him, still not as black as he
is sometimes painted. His criticism of things as they
are, the attitude that the majority always has been, is,
and will be wrong. Hence not to be taken too seriously.
Attitude toward America I don't in the least resent, as
it furnishes him subject matter for some of his most
sparkling wit.

I am aware of your characterization of a free library as an institution "to fuddle the imaginations,"
but perhaps you would feel more kindly to a library
run on Shavian principles by the four librarians
numbered among your readers. A bookbinder, reader
of *A Devil's Disciple*, will bind worn library books,
including your own much used volumes.

The group of readers that keep the wheels of trade
revolving is not lacking: Six general salesmen and
one each of clothing, oil and musical instruments,
and two life insurance agents; 5 salesladies, one department store manager, two advertising men, a
window trimmer, two commercial artists, two credit
men, an employment agent's wife, and a collector of
accounts due. The last has some interesting things
to say:

Shaw being never notorious for publicity dodging, I
was for a long while able to "get by" simply by echoing

his quips in the news. But in some book on the medical profession I was infected with a germ-stimulus which gave me no rest until I had read *The Doctor's Dilemma.*

Next I read *The Intelligent Woman's Guide, Man and Superman, The Apple Cart* and *Saint Joan.* Those I saw played were *Pygmalion* and *The Apple Cart.* The latter play I read after seeing.

Of the plays seen I liked *The Apple Cart* best. Of those read, *Saint Joan,* and that because he treated Joan with more sympathy than others I have read. *The Intelligent Woman's Guide* holds an honorable position on my shelves.

At no time do I really dislike Shaw, but if he would cut his intolerably long prefaces down to half, he would please me immensely. It would be futile to so hope— Shaw is not interested in pleasing anyone but himself; and so he will go on over-salting his popcorn and sparing the butter, underrating his readers' intelligence and overrating their endurance.

But I regret no time spent with Bernard Shaw— will visit with him again and see such of his plays as come. I agree with him often enough, now that I know any man writing in an epigrammatic style must, for cleverness sake, often be insincere. But because he *is* sincere at least as often as he can, and can, when he chooses, take other men's material and make it sing, I bow to him.

I do not question Shaw's indictment of the doctrine of laisser-faire, but I cannot share, as I once did, his enthusiasm for Socialism. Utopia is a pleasant place and many roads are reputed to lead there. I doubt if any of them do and the better paved entrance to Shaw's road does not lead me to make an exception of him. No, I'm afraid that for a practicable social philosophy I would do better to listen to Stuart Chase.

I know it has been said, in other words, that Shaw keeps America on the fire to boil his own pot, but his criticism of us is largely deserved. As an internationalist

I cannot in the least resent his shoving under our
noses things we would rather not smell. I would like
to believe that we could thus be stirred to eliminate some
of the evils to which we have become so accustomed.
But as a sceptic I expect nothing more of the bulk of my
compatriots than a holding of the nose while they
indignantly remind Shaw of our inherent superiority to
the English.

In a Shaw colony entertainers would certainly be
in demand, and they are not lacking from your
readers, who include a radio announcer, a radio
service man, a musician, and the wife of another, an
organist, two music teachers, a manager of a theater,
and an actress who had been reading *Androcles and
the Lion, Overruled* and *Pygmalion.*

Even in a Shaw colony there should not be lacking
the official representatives of religion, tho there is
only one minister, a reader of *John Bull's Other
Island* and *Major Barbara.* You have honored
ministers so frequently, if not favorably, in using
them as characters in your plays that it seems a pity
that they have not become better acquainted with
Anthony Anderson, the Presbyterian divine in *The
Devil's Disciple,* the Rev. James Mavor Morell in
Candida, and Mr. Rankin, the missionary, in *Capt.
Brassbound's Conversion,* not to mention others of
your religious characters. In addition to the lone
minister, religious representatives among your readers
are a Catholic sister, who had been reading *The
Devil's Disciple,* a Deaconess, a church secretary, who
had been reading two of your religious plays,
Androcles and the Lion and *Saint Joan,* two Y.M.C.A.

secretaries and the wife of one, who thus expresses herself:

I first became interested in Shaw's writings while taking graduate work in Columbia University. My interest in his plays was aroused by a series of lectures on contemporary drama. *The Apple Cart* is the only dramatic production which I have seen. I have read *Caesar and Cleopatra, Arms and the Man, Candida, Man and Superman, Back to Methuselah, Fanny's First Play, Pygmalion,* parts of *Saint Joan* and *The Intelligent Woman's Guide to Socialism.*

Man and Superman, Fanny's First Play, and *Caesar and Cleopatra* stand out most clearly. I enjoy the delightful wit, the penetrating wisdom, and the irreverent treatment of familiar legends. *The Intelligent Woman's Guide to Socialism* irked me most. It seems too easy to sit in England and blandly state that all American women are ignorant. That attitude spoiled the book for me.

Shaw impresses me as a profound student, as a man of brilliant wit, and of unusual conversational ability, as well as an outstanding example of irreverence and rudeness. There is so much that is mentally stimulating in his works that I do not worry over his bad manners unduly. The Introduction to *Back to Methuselah* gives my mind material to chew on for days, and his flashing wit gives me a feeling of laughing in my mind. I do not resent his criticism of things as they are for, even tho I do not always agree, his views stimulate my thinking.

His attitude toward America seems too superior to be healthy, but I dare say we need it. I am just as convinced that the English are imperfect as I am that we are. When foreigners consign us complacently to Limbo, I am reminded of a saying of my Grandmother's: "Said the sieve to the needle, 'You have a hole in your head.'"

In our Shaw colony death will come to some, and an undertaker is provided, a reader of *Saint Joan*, and an embalmer, a reader of *Androcles and the Lion*, *Overruled*, and *Pygmalion*.

Those of our colony who can indulge themselves will find among Shaw readers provision for luxurious tastes in a jeweler, a designer of jewelry, a diamond setter, an art dealer, a photographer and a lady's companion.

Among Shaw readers we find the unemployed, numbering 27, in whose reading nearly all of your writings are represented, including *The Intelligent Woman's Guide to Socialism*.

A Shaw colony certainly would want the news of the world, and among your readers the purveyors of news are especially well represented in three reporters, an editorial writer, the wife of a special feature writer, a writer with no other designation, a proof reader, a representative of the Associated Press, and two printers. Three of these have written letters to be quoted in part. The proof reader says:

I first became acquainted with Shaw thru reading his comments in the press. I noticed that they were usually sane, so sane that they aroused great opposition from those who blindly hold that this is the best of all possible worlds. I noticed that he was quite generally condemned by those who knew him only thru his impudent and provocative press utterances. I determined to know him better and set about to read his plays. I found them a well of pure delight. I learned that his press utterances gave a gravely distorted picture of the man.

If any of his plays have escaped me they are just trifles. I have seen played *Pygmalion, Saint Joan,*

Candida, and *The Apple Cart.* I have not yet read *The Apple Cart,* but will do so soon, as I expect it has a preface better than the play. *Pygmalion, You Never Can Tell, Androcles and the Lion* gave me the most pleasure. I cannot say that I disliked any of the plays, but *Back to Methuselah* and *Man and Superman* would probably be at the tail of the list. And let me add that I thought *The Revolutionist's Handbook* appended to *Man and Superman* splendid.

Shaw is something of an enigma. Mainly, I think, because of his studied, provocative habits of writing and speech. He knows enough to be conscious that he is an inconsequential bubble in the great flood of the Life Force, but he also knows enough to know that he is a much larger and more lustrous bubble than common. Then his sense of humor delights in enraging those who believe a man should modestly cough when his talents are mentioned.

His indictment of things as they are is the main point in his greatness. As he said of Shakespeare that he had nothing to say but the grandest way in the world of saying it so he has a grand way of saying his message but *he* has one that the world might well heed. And what he says of America is far too mild, as current events are demonstrating only too clearly. And then he lands on the British just as forcibly as ever he does the Americans, which is a fact that should be considered. The history of man, taken by and large, is nothing of which we should be inordinately proud. He tells us so and we hate him for it.

I am 28 years old, am married, have one child three years old who is named Ray *Shaw,* don't belong to any church or political party.

A reporter states his point of view succinctly:

I first became interested in Shaw when I heard people more "literary high-brow" than I discussing him.

I have never seen any of his plays on the stage. I have read *Saint Joan, Man and Superman, The Apple Cart, Androcles and the Lion, Pygmalion,* and some others I cannot recall. His plays are all charming, and his prefaces even more delightful. I found *Androcles* most delightful.

I think Shaw personally is a big blusterer, not without a subtle effect in much of his admitted nonsense. I know of no one in the literary world who is of greater insight or more stimulating to the modern reader. You might judge that Shaw is my favorite writer. He is.

The Associated Press representative says:

Some of Shaw's plays happened to be in the library at home, and were read to me by my mother when I was quite small. The plays I have read are: *John Bull's Other Island, Major Barbara, How He Lied to Her Husband, Androcles and the Lion, Pygmalion, The Devil's Disciple, Caesar and Cleopatra, Captain Brass-bound's Conversion, Saint Joan, Anthony and Cleopatra,* and several others that I cannot remember the titles of.

The most outstanding of these are, to my opinion, *Major Barbara, Androcles and the Lion,* and *Pygmalion. Major Barbara* shows the futility of war, and shows that yet it is sometimes necessary. Shaw draws his characters with remarkable clearness, and usually they represent a certain type of person, as in *Major Barbara,* Lady Britomart, whom Shaw evidently wishes to represent a type of British society woman whom he severely ridicules for her selfishness and avarice. In *Androcles and the Lion,* Shaw seems to be rather contemptuous of Christianity at times, but champions the cause of Christ in others, as in the notes, I believe of *Androcles and the Lion. Pygmalion* is one of the funniest and strangest plays that I have ever read, and has a very odd angle in regard to the flower girl, which could have very well really happened.

As to Shaw himself, he is rather inconsistent in many ways, so that one does not know just what to think of his philosophy, if you might call it that. In spite of his many peculiarities, and strange ideas, I would say that he is one of the greatest, if not the greatest satirist, and playwright, in the world today.

In regard to Shaw's attitude toward America, he has poked fun at his own countrymen, and their form of government, about as much as he has at us, as shown in any one of his plays about Great Britain. He is right in some respects toward American methods of doing business. He claims that America is "money mad," and I heartily agree with him.

I am really hopeful that you will accept my invitation to join our colony and spend your last days among your American readers. We know that you know that the more you criticize us the better we like you. The conflicting opinions, as indicated in the letters quoted, should give the spice that you require for a happy life. The colony, I am thinking, will resemble remarkably your Elysian Hell in *Man and Superman*. At least, why not try our colony and perhaps you will prefer it even to Hell. By the way, if in your opinion the colony needs a banker, bring one along with you, for American bankers have mostly failed and among your 431 readers there is not one banker.

Yours for Shavian Colonization,
A LIBRARIAN FROM MISSOURI

WHO READS WILLIAM JAMES?

Most of the enthusiasms of youth do not live in full vigour thru middle age, but occasionally one does. My enthusiasm for William James dates from my senior year in college, when his textbook on psychology and especially the chapter on habit made a profound impression on me. It stands out with more vividness now than any other college experience. Ever since college days I have been eager to know more about the man. His writings have interested me, but not as much, perhaps, as the man himself. I have often said that of all Americans the two that I should like most to have seen are Mark Twain and William James.

For the last twenty years I have been sharing this enthusiasm with others and within recent years I have been trying diligently to find some one who had read anything by James who did not respond in enthusiasm for him. We know that he had his opponents in philosophy, but it is a quality largely apart from his philosophy which makes this almost universal appeal. Recently I have been making a study of the readers of his books as they are circulated from the public library of one of our large American cities. His readers today, twenty-four years after his death, extend far beyond college walls and outside the homes of college graduates. An examination of his books, which happened one day to be on the shelves of the library, brought out some interesting facts as to present-day readers of James. None of the records go back farther than three years. They would, I think, interest James himself in showing how his philosophy is slowly permeating the masses.

I wrote letters to some of these readers of James's works, asking how they happened to be interested in him and the answers I received will be quoted in part later, but one needs no great imagination to take merely the list of names of readers and their occupations and build thereon a structure of ideals which James is creating in the minds of these men and women, plainly from the ordinary, common, everyday strata of society.

One would expect to find among readers of *Human Immortality* a minister, as in fact one does, indeed two of them, one white and one Negro. Would one, however, expect a trunk maker or a machinist or a stenographer to be interested in two supposed objections to the doctrine of human immortality, when it would be so much more practical for any one of them to read from the bountiful supply of library books on how to make a success of life and increase one's salary? Also among the readers of *Human Immortality* are a retired farmer, a clerk, three wives, two of physicians and one of a salesman, and lastly a postoffice employe whom perhaps one can hardly blame for hankering after something better than his present life.

Readers of James's books more strictly on philosophy are of an equally wide variety, but there is not a high-brow among them. I enjoy imagining the one who designates herself as a saleslady in a Ready to Wear Clothing store struggling with *A Pluralistic Universe* and pondering on the problems of the absolute as she sells gowns to the more materialistically inclined of her sex. Or let us imagine the chiropractor, as he manipulates the vertebrae of a patient, letting his mind wander off into the realms of the rival claims of pluralism and monism.

Among others who have been reading *A Pluralistic Universe*, *Pragmatism* and *Some Problems of Philosophy* are a printer, a probation officer of the Negro race, two mechanics, several salesmen, the wife of a real estate dealer, an artist and a number of teachers and students. The latter having used the books, probably as required readings in school courses, have little significance from our point of view. On the other hand I especially enjoy contemplating the woman employed in a laundry office, in her workday checking in bundles of soiled clothes and checking out bundles of clean shirts, collars and rough dry, but in the evening reading *Some Problems of Philosophy*, which was James's last book and expressed his latest philosophical viewpoint, altho published in incomplete form following his death. She would undoubtedly understand little if any of it, but there are therein those incomparable sentences of James which not unlikely would bring a thrill of joy to one in such restricted environment. Two sentences thus thrilled me. Perhaps they did the laundry worker.

Philosophy rouses us from our native dogmatic slumber and breaks up our caked prejudices.

A man with no philosophy in him is the most inauspicious and unprofitable of all possible social mates.

Caked prejudices, hardened like concrete and no philosophy in them, will account for most of the Babbitts and for many of the ills of mankind, local and international.

James has expressed the same thought beautifully in *On Some of Life's Ideals*:

No outward changes of condition in life can keep the nightingale of its eternal meaning from singing in all sorts of different men's hearts. This is the main fact to remember. If we could not only admit it with our lips but really and truly believe it, how our convulsive insistencies, how our antipathies and dreads of each other would soften down.

There are all sorts of men and women who have been reading *On Some of Life's Ideals* and *Talks to Teachers*, the most popularly written of James's works and the most widely read. These books constitute largely his lectures one year at Chautauqua, of which he writes so amusingly in his *Letters*. Let us observe this array of readers as they return their books to the desk at the library. I shall introduce them to you one by one by the nomenclature which they used on their application blanks when they registered to borrow books. First comes a laborer from a large factory of electrical goods, next a maintenance man at a soap factory, a student at an exclusive school for girls, a lawyer (the only lawyer listed among all those listed as readers of James), a clerk in a wholesale dry goods company, several teachers and several college students, a Negro teacher and a Negro high school student, a Negro salesman, a piano teacher, two physicians and a Bible class of an African Methodist Episcopal church, a clerk in a small grocery, a newspaper reporter, two social workers and a bond salesman. I like to think of William James speaking as it were with a radio from eternity his message of understanding and tolerance to such as these at a time when understanding and tolerance are much needed.

To me the most human of James's books and the most interesting outside of his *Letters* is his *Varieties of Religious Experience,* but strange as it may seem the range of its readers whose names were taken from the library records is limited to college students and one dealer in municipal bonds. This is probably largely a matter of chance, as this book had a large sale and was widely read. My letter of inquiry brought an answer from one of the students who had read a number of James's books, having become interested thru college courses in psychology and philosophy. It is interesting in its comments on *Varieties of Religious Experience.* This young man from his name and from an idealism running thru his letter—an idealism so common to his race—I judge to be a Jew. He says:

Varieties of Religious Experience is perhaps one of the best single books ever written on any single phase of social psychology. This sage, partial to no sect yet deeply religious, with dazzling brilliancy turns the revealing light of psychology upon religion. There is no partial creed feeling, no gloomy pessimism, nor for that matter rosy optimism to mar the unsurpassed psychology

of James. The empiricism of the scientist which is
interested in a fact merely because it is a fact is, in
James, tempered by the philosophic attitude which
demands to know the import of facts.

The *Letters of William James*, incomparable in
all the qualities which make letters dear to those like
myself who are especially fond of them, attracted
readers of much the same kind as his other books.
They included a young woman in an advertising and
insurance office who, I judge, did not read the *Letters*
for anything she could glean on filing systems or on
business letter writing. Also among the readers of
the *Letters* were a woman employed by a dredging
company, a bond salesman, the same that read
Varieties of Religious Experience, the wife of another
bond man, and, lastly, a laborer by the name of Tony
with a surname as plainly Italian, employed by a large
clay products company. He lived on what is known
as Dago Hill and how he came to find out anything
about William James would be interesting to know.
I wrote to him but received no reply. Perhaps he has
returned to Italy's sunny shores. He would undoubtedly find pleasure in the following in one of
James's letters :

Today in Italy my spirits have riz. The draggle-
tailed physiognomy of the railway stations on the way
here, the beautifully good-natured, easy-going expression
on the faces of the railway officials, the charming
dialog I have just had with the aged but angelic chamber-
maid whose phrases I managed to understand without
recognizing any particular words—all let me go to bed
with a light heart.

The young Jewish student from whose letter I have already quoted writes feelingly regarding James's *Letters*:

> To read the *Letters of William James* is to indulge in a real pleasure; it is to read something more entertaining than the best fiction ever written; it is to introduce one's self to the greatest of personalities: kind, gentle and wholesouled, warm, genial and courteous, a dazzling intellect combined with unobtrusive modesty, one who is blessed with a delicate but keen sense of humor, an idealist but not a dreamer, a philosopher but not a dogmatist, a scientist but not a doctrinaire.
>
> One cannot know psychology without knowing James; one cannot read James without knowing him; one cannot know him without being strongly attracted to him.

From some of the other letters received from readers of William James I have selected a few extracts. A young man engaged in selling musical instruments writes:

> My reading of James has been the natural result of an interest in philosophy and psychology. Altho lacking a university-trained mind, I nevertheless in a humble way can appreciate the master in James. In his *Human Immortality*, his sympathetic understanding of the hope of mankind, combined with a rare scientific insight, gives the book its charm and convincing qualities. However, the book that brings these qualities out prominently is *Varieties of Religious Experience*.

An employe in one of the city offices writes:

> After going thru his book on *The Will to Believe*, it left a profound impression on me. I found it inspiring, logical and nutritious. His book on Habit's re-education

of the mind is good, also the energies of men. His book on religious experiences was uplifting and edifying. His article on the sick soul was really a description of himself. He like myself had only a small store of energy. His ideal of life was to keep the mind always filled with thoughts of the good, the beautiful and the true. His books as I turned from page to page revealed my own inner weaknesses. He showed how to strengthen the inner life, making calmness an ideal free from passion, anger, selfishness and hatred. He showed how the mind can carry you to the heights in self confidence if you have the will to believe.

An artist writes:

While I am not a student of this famous American philosopher's writings I have derived much pleasure and instruction from reading some of his lectures. It is his general tone of common sense, in addition to his masterly exposition of facts, his unbiased philosophical view of the nature of the universe, his broad gauge. I had no special reason for reading a *Pluralistic Universe* except that I am an admirer of all sound writings. In the writings of William James I found much to clarify the mind and to clean out the cobwebs of fear, superstition, etc. and he assisted me to think logically and not theologically.

The writer of the next letter characterizes himself as twenty-five years of age, white, single, something of an idealist, tho fairly practical, interested in ideas about people rather than people themselves.

You ask how I happened to be interested in *Problems of Philosophy*. Merely because James wrote it. You see, I've somehow acquired the conception of James as one of the outstanding figures in contemporary thought. (Partly from the opinions of others, and partly from things of his I have read, I suppose.) I can't discuss very intelligently the book you ask about, for I had merely looked at it a few times before the library began sending me a series of vigorous notes, telling me it was past due.

I had—and have—the intention of reading about all of James that I could; but business leaves one's ambition rather enervated. If I can get some kind of a hold on the important things that have been written by James and a few others—Havelock Ellis, for instance—it will be better than reading aimlessly here and yon, it seems to me.

My admiration for James comes chiefly, I think, from his wonderful ability to write. Ellis, it is said, writes in a manner "at once intimate and grand." I wish I had thought of that to say of James. I believe it would have then been even truer.

James's style fascinates me particularly because I hope to learn some day a little of his art. At present I am doing a very elementary sort of writing: reporting for trade publications. But, nevertheless, I know good work when I see it. It's like a fiddler in a cheap theatre listening to Kreisler.

These extracts are used, not because they give any new points of view regarding James, but because they represent the general customary opinion of readers on his books. The hundred or so readers of James whose records I have examined are undoubtedly typical of other readers of James in this library and of readers of his works thruout the country. They come largely of the common, substantial men and women to whom James so often paid reverence. "Divinity lies all about us, and culture is too hidebound to even suspect the fact." Most of them probably do not have much formal education, but they are thinkers and dreamers. It may largely be desultory reading which they are doing but it is reading which they are doing for the joy of it. An examination of the records of the readers of books of other authors of solid and substantial qualities, whether the field be philosophy, economics, religion or science, would undoubtedly reveal readers of the same kind as those of William James. I hope some day the illusion will be dispelled that public libraries for the most part circulate only fiction and that of the lightest variety. Perhaps the most striking fact in a library survey of the readers of books of more serious import would be the comparatively small number from business and the professions. A further indication of the increasing popular demand for serious reading is the recent amazing growth of the movement for adult education which has been sponsored in England and America by the workers and shows an encouraging ferment in their mental and intellectual development. It is a movement which our so-called more cultured classes might well emulate.

WHO READS THE GREEK CLASSICS TODAY?

As Homer was reclining one day in the halls of Pluto in Hades, he tuned in with his radio and got a station somewhere in the United States. A university president was on the air. He said: "Today education is practical. At the institution of which I have the honor to be the head there is hardly a vocation from auto mechanics to dressmaking for which we cannot prepare you. Thank God, the time when a student takes a classical education is gone forever. Homer is dead."

At the last remark Homer sat up and took notice. "Can it be true," he said, "that I am dead after being an immortal for all of these many centuries? I shall immediately call Aeschylus, Sophocles, and Euripides and we shall take off for this country called the United States."

This he did and Aristophanes came along with the other three, asserting his right to accompany them. To this they assented, tho not without some misgiving. They were all of one mind, however, that they did not desire the company of Socrates, Plato, Aristotle, and the other philosophers who were always messing things up with their metaphysics.

Homer led the way, Charon piloted them safely over the Styx, and they made a safe and rapid flight to the United States. The first thing to do, they agreed, was to look up this university president and ask him what he had in mind when he asserted that Homer was dead. They found him without trouble. He confirmed their worst fears. His university had long since dropped Greek from the curriculum—the students had more useful subjects to pursue. The president, however, invited them to the faculty club for lunch and they heard many subjects discussed and many names mentioned, but never the far famed Attica nor any of its heroes. They mingled among the students and at first they got a gleam of encouragement for they heard two of them speak certain letters of the Greek alphabet. However, they discovered later that they were merely discussing a basket ball game between the Phi Deltas and the Sigma Chis.

They shook off the dust of their feet in the halls of learning and turned to the abodes of the professions. Here, too, they found they were unknown, for the lawyers were disputing among themselves, the doctors saving lives, the priests saving souls, the engineers building bridges, and the scientists solving riddles. Not one of them cared for the Greek classics, if he had ever heard of them.

Homer, Aeschylus, Sophocles, and Euripides were by this time thoroly disheartened, but Aristophanes merely laughed and said he now knew enough about America to write a play that would put the *Frogs* and the *Clouds* and his other plays in the shade and he was going to write it immediately upon his return to Hades.

The five of them were walking along the street when they came to a Greek Temple. To them there could be no mistake: it was a Greek Temple with graceful columns, classic facade, inscriptions. They entered to bring offerings to Aegis-bearing Zeus, to Pallas Athene, and to Phoebus Apollo. Here they found not the altars of their gods for they had come within the walls of a public library. Their mistake was not surprising, for public library buildings in America are not unlike Greek temples. When our visitors from Hades made themselves known, the librarian explained to them what a public library was. Like modern writers, they immediately wanted to know whether their complete works were on the shelves and at first they were indignant to find so few of them in the catalog, not realizing that many had been lost during the vaunted progress of civilization. They were pleased, however, to discover themselves translated into the languages of many barbarian nations.

The librarian took them to the Greek alcove and showed them their works in all these languages. Then he told them he was delighted to have them come at this opportune time for he had recently been making an investigation of the readers of their works and he knew he had some facts that would surprise and please them. Homer need not fear that he was going to die for the Odyssey and the Iliad were being read daily by the hoi polloi, and the works of the other gentlemen were also popular. The delegation from Hades evinced interest and the librarian told them this story.

"I attended college when the study of Greek was as yet considered the highest of intellectual pursuits. I had no special aptitude for it tho I pursued it for six years and became acquainted with all of you and acquired a love for you which remains with me to this day. Recently I watched the ashes of my Greek teacher sprinkled on the roots of an oak tree planted in his honor on the grounds of my alma mater—old Greek that he was, straight and lithe body, ruddy brown face, and hair like lances in a phalanx, every one bristling with independence and individuality. There has been stamped even more indelibly upon my mind a picture of this man sitting at his desk with "A Reading From Homer" on the wall behind him, instructing us, untutored sons of virgin soil, in Greek beauty and greatness. Our admiration for him was tempered with a fear of those shafts of satire and irony with which he brought us low when we came to class unprepared. His spirit must be seeking you out now for he is not long dead. I cannot imagine him in other than Hades—certainly not in a heaven of harps and halos and hallelujahs. Perhaps due to memory of him, recently I decided to find out for myself whether Greek literature was rapidly dying or whether, breaking thru the walls like the light of Phoebus Apollo, it has permeated the homes of the unlettered.

"I looked up the records in the library of about one hundred recent readers of your works. In your day they would have been slaves; today they are free but they do the common, ordinary work of the world as it is carried on now. Many are the new

occupations since your day and I shall not take the
time to explain them to you. Like the catalog of
ships in the Iliad, I shall now bring these readers
before you. Will you be proud that such a motley
array should come as it were to listen to the bards
recite Homer or the actors and the chorus give the
plays of you, Aeschylus, Sophocles, Euripides, and
Aristophanes? First come the readers of the Iliad
to take their place in the agora. Among them are
seen a printer, an accountant, a salesman, two clerks,
a cabinet-maker from Ethiopia, two bookkeepers, two
architectural draftsmen, a stenographer, an Ethiopian
insurance agent, a hospital attendant, two musicians,
one from a vaudeville theatre. To them, O Homer,
I inscribe these of your words:

> So speaking, to the arms of his dear spouse
> He gave the boy; she on her fragrant breast
> Received him, weeping as she smiled. The chief
> Beheld, and, moved with tender pity, smoothed
> Her forehead gently with his hand and said:

> "Sorrow not thus, beloved one, for me.
> No living man can send me to the shades
> Before my time; no man of woman born,
> Coward or brave, can shun his destiny.
> But go thou home, and tend thy labors there—
> The web, the distaff—and command thy maids
> To speed the work. The cares of war pertain
> To all men born in Troy, and most to me."

> Thus speaking, mighty Hector took again
> His helmet, shadowed with the horse-hair plume,
> While homeward his beloved consort went,
> Oft looking back, and shedding many tears!

"Next come readers of the Odyssey, among whom we find a hair-dresser from Ethiopia, a saleslady and a salesman, a field engineer, a printer, a modern chariot driver, an advertising solicitor, an ad writer, a nurse, and several wives of men of similar occupations. For these I should like to quote the words of the fair-robed Nausicaa:

"Papa dear, could you not have the wagon harnessed for me—the high one, with good wheels—to take my nice clothes to the river to be washed, which now are lying dirty? Surely for you yourself it is but proper, when you are with the first men holding councils, that you should wear clean clothing. Five good sons too are here at home—two married, and three merry young men still—and they are always wanting to go to the dance wearing fresh clothes. And this is all a trouble on my mind."

Such were her words, for she was shy of naming the glad marriage to her father; but he understood it all, and answered thus:

"I do not grudge the mules, my child, nor anything beside. Go! Quickly shall the servants harness the wagon for you, the high one, with good wheels, fitted with rack above."

"You are not soaring on Mount Olympus in this passage, O Homer, but you have struck a chord in the human breast to which you can be sure these readers responded.

"The group of readers of Aeschylus and Sophocles is not so large nor does it offer such a wide variety of occupations. It includes a stenographer, a commercial artist, the wife of a railroad foreman, a salesman, a book agent, a piano teacher, two book-keepers, a college professor, the wife of a mechanic,

and several youths.   These words of yours, O
Aeschylus, in *Prometheus Bound* must have made the
blood course more rapidly thru their veins as they
viewed the grandeur of your picture of a god's
sacrifice for man:

> Ay! in act now, in word now no more,
>   Earth is rocking in space.
> And the thunders crash up with a roar upon roar,
>   And the eddying lightnings flash fire in my face,
> And the whirlwinds are whirling the dust round and
>   round,
>   And the blasts of the winds universal leap free,
> And blow each upon each with a passion of sound,
>   And aether goes mingling in storm with the sea.
> Such a curse on my head, in a manifest dread,
>   From the hand of your Zeus has been hurled along.
> O my mother's fair glory! O Aether, enringing
>   All eyes with the sweet common light of thy
>   bringing!
> Dost see how I suffer this wrong?

"And you, Oh Sophocles, in your understanding
of the toughness of the human spirit under calamity,
you, too, must have moved these simple folk profoundly in such words as those of the Chorus in
Oedipus at Colonus:

> For when youth passes with its giddy train,
> Troubles on troubles follow, toils on toils,
>   Pain, pain, forever pain;
>   And none escapes life's coils.
>   Envy, sedition, strife,
> Carnage and war, make up the tale of life.
> Last comes the worst and most abhorred stage
>   Of unregarded age,
> Joyless, companionless and slow,
>   Of woes the crowning woe.

"The readers of Euripides make up a large, varying group. They include a drug store clerk, an accountant, several teachers, a steam fitter, an adjuster, an inspector, the wife of a furniture dealer, a beauty specialist, a butcher, the wife of a brakeman, two bookkeepers, two architects, a clerk, a telephone operator, two accountants, a doctor's wife, a news writer, a piano teacher, and the wife of a manufacturer of labels.

"You, O Euripides, if I may be permitted to say so, are the most human and perhaps the most modern of the company with which I am now being honored, and I know that these readers have been able to understand you, for you speak in their language and you treat of the emotions, the loves and hates, which now as in your time drive men hither and thither like the elements of nature unleashed in a storm. Your character, Hippolytus, is not unlike our hero, Lindbergh, who was more fortunate than Icarus in crossing the sea. You can be sure that Medea's hate, the tigress cruelty, the mother's fierce love for her children moved these readers. Medea discarded by Jason for a younger woman, banished from her home—how modern! How terrible was her revenge! Women born to tears, as you say. The words of Medea, as she prepared to kill her own children lest they fall into the hands of her enemies, must have burned themselves into these, your readers:

"O me accurst in this my desperate mood!
For naught, for naught, my babes, I nurtured you,
And all for naught I laboured, travail-worn,
Bearing sharp anguish in your hour of birth.

Ah for the hopes—unhappy!—all mine hopes
Of ministering hands about mine age,
Of dying folded round with loving arms,
All men's desire! But now—'tis past—'tis past,
That sweet imagining! Forlorn of you
A bitter life and woeful shall I waste.
Your mother never more with loving eyes
Shall ye behold, passed to another life.
Woe! woe! why gaze your eyes on me, my darlings?"

"To you, Aristophanes, I cannot report so many readers. Perhaps you are considered rather naughty, but more likely your jokes, being so local in their application, are not so well understood today. Among your readers, however, there are a manufacturer of glue, an insurance agent, the wife of a salesman, an English teacher, two youths, a peddler, and an electrician.

"In making this investigation of readers I was not satisfied," said the librarian, "until I wrote to some of them to find out whether they really had an appreciation of Greek literature or were merely reading to acquire superficial culture. I am giving you a few extracts from some of the letters received. The first is from an insurance man who says:

It would be a very difficult matter for me to tell why, or exactly when, I became interested in the classics, but I presume it happened in this way. I was born and reared on a Kansas farm. When a boy a Carnegie Library was opened at Manhattan, about ten miles from my home. I used to bring a load of wood or produce to town, sell it, and then spend the remainder of the day at the free library. On one of my trips I found Plutarch's *Lives*, took it home and, figuratively speak-

ing, devoured it. History had always been my favorite
study, but of course in the country school only modern
history, and no philosophy, had been taught and the
Lives opened up for me a field of ancient history in
which I have roamed ever since. However, I have no
special preference for the Greek Classics.

My hobby is Archeology; I read everything I can
get on the accomplishments of man, whether as a
savage or a so-called civilized creature. You found at
the library that I had taken out Greek Classics, but
you might also have found that it is only one of the
branches of my reading. I am particularly fond of
natural philosophy as taught by the various schools of
Greek thought. The outlook on life of such men as
Socrates, Plato, and in fact all of the best known Greek
teachers, including the poets, even tho their writings
contain varying opinions, seems to me much superior to
our present day dogmatic forms of religion teaching
of a God as nearly anthropomorphic as those gods
rejected by the men under discussion.

The freedom of these men from the necessity of
complying with formulas of worship and the lack of
necessity of worship of a god at all left their minds open
to mental contemplation and investigation not permitted
under our present social system. I love the Greek
classics because with them only, it seems to me, am I
able to find the real thoughts of men, free from
opinions previously conceived and taught. They were
the first Original Thinkers.

"This letter from a commercial artist is given in
full because, of all the letters, it best represents what
the Greek masters in literature bring to the thought-
ful man in the complexities of modern life:

Knowing well the weakness of the average reader
of the Greek Classics for an over-idealization of the

Greeks, I shall try to use some restraint in telling you
why I am interested in the culture of another age.

To me, life has grown too complex and aimless.
But, there must be, by the law of averages, a great deal
of beauty today, altho I confess I am not able always
to discover it in the general confusion of jazz, sex,
cheap sentimentality, and publicity.

However, modern life has not driven me to read
the Classics. Rather, the Classics have helped me to
tolerate modern life. Thru them I have learned to
treasure simplicity, restraint, and order. When I was
quite a child I felt the power and beauty of the
characters and deeds of Achilles and the heroes of the
Trojan war. Later I felt the same power in the straight
lines of Greek architecture and the subordination of
detail in their sculpture. Then, in the Greek literature I
saw these great people, vigorous and natural. Even
Greek names are forceful. Clytemnestra!

I am not a student of the Classics. . . . Twelve years
ago I graduated from high school and there my "education" stopped, so, you can see, my interest is not one of
schooling.

I dislike the word "student" which implies a certain
critical seriousness—I don't like to "paw" over the
Classics. I prefer to accept them as I imagine the great
body of Greeks did—as part of my natural existence.

"The following is from a hospital librarian:

To tell how I became interested in the Greek Classics,
I must go back to my early childhood when *Tooke's
Pantheon* at my mother's knee was the most absorbing
and delightful of books.

I hope I may go back to the enjoyment again of
good translations of the old classics and that I will like
them even better in my elderly years than when I met
them first so long ago.

"A letter from a newspaper writer shows a fine appreciation and understanding of Greek literature and thought:

I was brought up on the Greek stories. I knew Perseus and Medea and Theseus when I was in pinafores. I was not neglected on the German and French fairy stories that are the mainstay of our folklore but I always liked the Greek stories. I don't know Greek altho I did the customary amount of schoolboy translating as far as Homer. But it has seemed to me that the ancients of any race I have ever heard about were not so astonishingly different from the moderns of any age you like to choose. So it came about quite naturally that I enjoyed the Greek plays when I came to an age to enjoy if not to appreciate them with the scholar's appreciation. I have been reading them when the mood touched me these forty years. Euripides seems nearer the moderns than any of the others who covered the Agamemnon stories. You have doubtless noticed— the observation is not original—how humanly he treats the attitude of Orestes and his sister after the murder of Clytemnestra in contrast to the grim fateful tone of Sophocles, for instance. And in the Knights you may recall that the political go-getter tucks a cushion under Mr. Common People with a joke as broad as Mademoiselle from Armentières. I can't recall them off-hand but it is amusing to note how many of the jokes of Marathon and Salamis were like the jokes of the great war—most of them jokes that are not told in any but selected—not select—company by the soldiers of that campaign; it is no trick to find them.

I am not a student so you will have to go elsewhere for learned comparisons and lofty thoughts. I have none to offer that fall in that category. But the Greeks, especially Aristophanes, were too human ever to die."

When the librarian finished reading from these letters, his guests thanked him and departed happier in that they now knew there was little danger that men would ever forget them. The librarian watched the immortals as they left the building and then resumed his more customary duties of handing out best sellers to his reading public, comforted in his own mind, however, by the discerning few who preferred his beloved Greek writers.

INDEX TO LETTERS FROM READERS